For Margaret, with love—
and for Christopher Lord, Roger Cooper, and Russell Taylor,
in memory of Budapest, October–November 1956

Old men forget: yet all shall be forgot,
But he'll remember, with advantages,
What feats he did that day.

—Henry V, *act 4, scene 3*

I read but few lives of great men because biographers do not, as a rule, tell enough about the formative period of life. What I want to know is what a man did as a boy.

—*Ulysses S. Grant*

Ulysses S. Grant

CHAPTER

1

In the summer of 2003 Ulysses S. Grant made news all across the country that he had, in his lifetime, done so much to reunite: Some of his descendants, a good part of the more serious press, and the Grant Monument Association objected strongly to pop diva Beyoncé Knowles, accompanied by a "troupe of barely clad dancers," using his tomb in New York City's Riverside Park as the background for a raucous, "lascivious," nationally televised July Fourth concert.[1]

Beyoncé and her fans hardly seemed aware of who Grant was, or why such a fuss should be made about the presence of loud music, suggestive dancing, partial nudity, and a huge, boisterous crowd in front of his tomb, which, as the *New York Times* pointed out, had once been a bigger tourist attraction than the Statue of Liberty. In fact, except for a few members of the Grant family who had been trying for years to get the bodies of General Grant and his wife, Julia, removed from the tomb on the grounds that it had been allowed to fall into a disgraceful state of repair and decay, the level of public indignation was low. The *Times* even felt compelled to comment rather sniffily that the general was "no longer the immensely famous figure he once was." Grant's great-grandson Chapman Foster Grant, then fifty-eight, however, took a different view of Beyoncé's concert, commenting, "Who knows? If the old guy were alive, he might have liked it."

Knowing as much as we do about the general's relationship with Mrs.

Grant—like President Lincoln, whom he much admired, Grant was notoriously devoted to a wife who felt herself and her family to be vastly socially superior to his and was not shy about letting her opinion on the subject be known; and, like Mrs. Lincoln, Mrs. Grant's physical charms, such as they may have been, were lost on everybody but her dutiful husband—it seems unlikely that Grant would have allowed himself to appreciate Beyoncé's presence at his tomb. Mrs. Grant, it was generally felt, kept her husband on a pretty tight leash when it came to pretty girls, barely clothed or not.

As for Grant himself, while he had his problems with liquor—his reputation as a drinker is perhaps the one thing that most Americans still remember about him, that and the fact that his portrait, with a glum, seedy, withdrawn, and slightly guilty expression, like that of a man with a bad hangover, is on the fifty-dollar bill—no allegation of any sexual indiscretion blots his record. He reminds one, in fact, of Byron's famous lines about George III:

> *He had that household virtue, most uncommon,*
> *Of constancy to a bad, ugly woman.*

Grant not only led a blameless domestic life, he was the very reverse of flamboyant. Softspoken, given to long silences, taciturn, easily hurt and embarrassed, he was the most unlikely of military heroes. He did not, like Gen. Ambrose Burnside, for example, who was so soundly defeated by Lee at Fredericksburg, lend his name to a style of swashbuckling full sidewhiskers—"sideburns," as they came to be known after him. Nor did he lend his name, as the unfortunate Gen. Joseph Hooker (who succeeded Burnside and was defeated by Lee at Chancellorsville) was thought to have done, to label the prostitutes who were said to surround his headquarters, so that even today they are still known as "hookers" by people who have never heard of the general himself. Grant aimed to be the most ordinary appearing and self-effacing of men, and to a very large extent he succeeded.

The fact that Beyoncé is black, as was much of the audience of thousands gathered to listen to her concert, might have shocked the general rather less than her near nudity or the "lascivious choreography" reported by the *Times*. Grant probably did more than anyone except Lincoln to destroy the institution of slavery in North America, but, like Lincoln, he shared the social attitude toward Negroes of his own race and his time. However, his innate good manners, natural courtesy, and a certain broadminded tolerance always marked his behavior toward them. It was typical of him that while very few other generals in that age would have had a Native American officer on their staffs, Grant did, and as president he deplored the way in which government agents exploited the Indians, seeming to have felt that Custer got what was coming to him at the Little Big Horn.

Grant's personal and professional opinion of Custer had always been low, and although he made more than his share of political and financial mistakes in the White House and afterward, and his judgment of character when it came to civilians was notoriously optimistic, his judgment of generalship was invariably ruthlessly objective and on target. Grant was unsure about a lot of things, but he knew a flashy, incompetent, and reckless general when he saw one, so Custer's defeat at the hands of Sitting Bull and Crazy Horse did not surprise or shock him, unlike the rest of the United States.

What he would have made of the Grant family's long struggle to extricate him and Mrs. Grant from Grant's Tomb as it fell into disrepair and decay and move them elsewhere is hard to say. One of the reasons the campaign failed was the question of where to put the Grants if they were removed from their tomb in New York City. With that mournful failure of judgment that was apt to come over Grant off the battlefield, he and Mrs. Grant chose New York City for their resting place, in part out of a dislike for Washington, D.C.—Grant's two terms as president had not produced in either of them any affection for Washington society, nor, in the end, was there much affection in Washington for them—while Galena, Illinois, which seemed too provincial a backwater in which to bury such a great man, had even fewer happy memories for the Grants than did Washington.

In Galena, having retired—as a captain, under a cloud—from the army in 1854, Grant had nursed a drinking problem that was the talk of the town, and was reduced to working as a clerk in his father's harness shop—a humiliation he felt keenly. Galena would not therefore have recommended itself to the Grants as the place to bury the most admired American general since Washington, and perhaps the greatest American of the nineteenth century.

Although Grant had been miserable at West Point, which he had never wanted to attend in the first place, he was tempted to choose it as the location for his tomb, but typically gave up on the idea when he realized that Mrs. Grant could not be buried beside him there. He had never been happy when separated from her for any length of time—hence the occasional drinking bouts—and he was not about to be buried without providing a place for her by his side.

Grant was always a sucker for other people's financial schemes, so it is hardly surprising that he was easily persuaded of the merits of the Upper West Side of New York, which was being touted in the late nineteenth century as the coming fashionable neighborhood of the city. Real estate developers pointed to the heights overlooking the Hudson River as the natural place for all that was wealthy and glamorous in New York Society to live, and indeed, for a time it seemed as if they were right, and that the Upper West Side would be New York's equivalent of Paris's sixteenth *arrondissement*, with the added advantage of a stunning river view. The site above the Hudson in Riverside Park, at Riverside Drive and West 122nd

Street, must have seemed like the ideal place for a mausoleum that was intended to rival Napoleon's, and which to this day remains the second largest in the Western world (the Garfield Memorial—oddly enough, considering that President Garfield's reputation is far more diminished than Grant's—is the largest).*

The "General Grant National Memorial,"[2] as it is officially known, would be built with donations from more than ninety thousand of his grateful fellow citizens, for a total of six hundred thousand dollars, the most money that had ever been raised for a public monument at the time, and more than a million people gathered to see his body conveyed there, in a procession that stretched for more than seven miles, contained sixty thousand marchers, and included President Grover Cleveland, two ex-presidents, the justices of the U. S. Supreme Court, and countless generals, including former Confederate generals Joseph E. Johnston and Simon Bolivar Buckner. No "lascivious choreography" was on display, needless to say.

The Grants can be forgiven for not being able to foresee the failure of the Upper West Side to deliver on its promise—after all, John D. Rockefeller, Jr., who was far shrewder, made the same mistake when he put Riverside Church there, as did William Randolph Hearst when he built an enormous penthouse apartment overlooking the Hudson—but there is a certain irony to the fact that but for their own resistance to the idea, Grant's Tomb could have been in Washington, D.C., close by the memorials to Washington, Jefferson, and Lincoln.

There, because of its high visibility, Grant's giant memorial, with its orderly rows of Doric columns, would no doubt have been lovingly preserved, pristine and gleaming, by the U.S. National Park Service, and lines of schoolchildren and tourists would be waiting to visit it even today.

*Grant, who seldom had anything bad to say about anyone, said about Garfield that "he possessed the backbone of an angleworm."

Instead it overlooks the West Side Highway, has been incongruously surrounded by a bright red serpentine wall—a hideous "community project"—and stands right smack in the middle of a neighborhood many New Yorkers still avoid as much as possible, given its reputation for drug dealing, gang warfare, racial tension, and muggings.

In memorials, as in every other aspect of real estate, location is everything, and the Grants were as unlucky in their choice of real estate as they were in their personal finances. A recent cleaning and rebuilding of Grant's Tomb (at a cost of nearly two million dollars) has at least gotten rid of most of the grime—and the vagrants who used it as a nesting place and a toilet. While some of the monument's more glaring structural problems have been solved, it still remains a rather shabby-looking place, well off the beaten track for the memorial to one of the most admired Americans of his day and the man who, of all American military commanders, best understood how to put the nation's overwhelming resources to work on the battlefield.

The fact that Grant gave the amount of thought that he did to his memorial is surprising, given his reputation for being unassuming, slovenly in personal appearance, modest, and easily put upon—modern biographers love to contrast Lee in his dress uniform, sash, and ornate sword at Appomattox with Grant, riding up late, mud-spattered and swordless in his "private's uniform," with only the shoulder bars bearing his three stars to distinguish him from an ordinary soldier—but like so much about Grant, this is a misleading image. Contemporary photographs of Grant certainly make it clear that he was not a "dressy" general, but he never wore a private's uniform. He seems to have favored a kind of dark blue suit, with a long coat and a waistcoat, bearing the gilt buttons of the U.S. Army and the regulation shoulder boards—a uniform, in fact, not unlike the one Lee generally wore except on ceremonial occasions, except that Lee's was gray. Certainly Grant did not usually wear a sword, but neither did Lee, who wore his at Appomattox only because he thought it would be his obligation to hand it over to Grant as a token of surrender.

This is, in fact, part of a widespread failure to understand Grant's character, which was admittedly complex and always, to some degree, secretive. With Lee what you saw was what you got—he was a proud, patrician officer, a *beau sabreur*, a born commander who expected to be obeyed. With Grant what you saw was what he wanted you to see—a plain, ordinary man with no pretensions to gentility or military glamour. But in truth Grant never saw himself as "plain" or "ordinary," and was always intensely conscious of his rank, his social position, and his gifts as a commander. Grant's black slouch hat, his omnipresent cigar, and his muddy boots are not so much a pose, like Ike's not wearing his medal ribbons on his uniform jacket, or Monty's affecting a beret, baggy corduroy trousers, and a sweater even as a field marshal, but rather a simple lack of interest in military niceties, a fierce concentration on the *business* of war—which is winning—rather than the display of war, which seemed to him a waste of time and energy.

It is no surprise that Grant suffered from that most unwarlike of maladies, migraine headaches—he worried about every detail, nothing he did as a general was casual, everything was meticulously calculated and thought out to bring about victory. Like the Duke of Wellington, Grant did not share his plans with his subordinates (or even with the president); he concentrated on a plan, worked it out in his head, fretted over the smallest details of supply and logistics, then waited (he would not be pushed, pressured, or hurried) for the right moment to put it into effect. As for Grant's taste for plain uniforms, it is worth remembering that although Wellington was an aristocrat and had himself painted innumerable times in the full uniform of a British field marshal with all his orders and decorations, he wore a plain dark frock coat and black cocked hat at Waterloo, with no gold lace or decorations. Grant was far from the only great general in history who had more on his mind than his appearance.

All the same, one of the qualities that comes across loud and clear in any account of Grant's life is his touchiness. It was not a question of vanity or personal pride so much as the fear on the part of a man who had always been underestimated as a boy and looked down on by people who assumed they were better than he was.

Grant, for all his slouchiness and apparent good nature, was not a man who forgave slights easily, if at all. Though he and Winfield Scott Hancock (the future Union general who would hold Cemetery Ridge against Pickett's Charge on the third day of Gettysburg) were roommates at West Point and had fought together as young officers in the Mexican War, Grant took Hancock's perceived failure to salute him properly in 1866 as "a personal snub." Afterward he maintained an attitude of harsh and prickly animosity toward Hancock until Grant's dying day, when Grant finally confessed that he regretted the pain he had caused Hancock.

Hancock was handsome, socially secure, a flamboyantly brilliant soldier, wealthy, and a famous ladykiller, all the things that Grant was not, which may have had something—possibly everything—to do with Grant's feelings about Hancock, but the fact remains that he was one of the very few people for whom Grant expressed an open dislike, among the others being Jefferson Davis, the former president of the Confederacy, and Custer. As a rule Grant nursed his grievances silently—although the same cannot be said of Mrs. Grant.[3]

In war Grant's reactions to those who attempted to impose on him were swift, sure, bleak, and when necessary, brutal. Indeed, his first serious dose of fame came in February 1862, when he responded to a courteous plea for terms of surrender sent to him under a flag of truce by his old West Point classmate and friend Simon Bolivar Buckner, whom Grant had besieged and surrounded at Fort Donelson, with a brief note that signaled to many people, among them President Lincoln, that here at last was a Union general who did not mince words and was not afraid to suffer casualties and close with the enemy. "No terms except unconditional and immediate surrender can be accepted," wrote Grant in brusque reply to Buckner. "I propose to move immediately upon your works."

Buckner later protested at these "ungenerous and unchivalrous terms," but he nevertheless promptly surrendered to Grant with nearly fifteen thousand Confederate troops and forty cannon, the first real Union victory in nine months of war, and one that caught the fancy of the American public because "unconditional surrender" mirrored Grant's initials, so that for a time he was known in the press as "Unconditional Surrender Grant."

If Buckner supposed that chivalry was a matter of concern to Grant, or that their old days together at West Point, or the fact that he had once loaned Grant money, would have a mellowing effect on Grant, he had misjudged his opponent badly. Grant was fair—he would be generous to a fault toward Lee at Appomattox—but chivalry, as Buckner should have known, played no part in his concept of war. For Grant, the least romantic of generals, the fastest way—indeed, the *only* way—to get the war over with was to fight and win. It went largely unnoticed at the time that Grant had suffered nearly three thousand casualties to two thousand on the Confederate side to win at Fort Donelson—casualties did not frighten Grant or shake his determination to fight, then or later.

Grant hated war, had no illusions about it, and disliked all attempts to disguise its brutality with chivalrous concepts or fancy uniforms. It was about killing, and he recognized from the very beginning of the war what few other Union generals were willing to face at the time, which was that there would have to be a whole lot of killing done—more than anybody on either side could possibly imagine—before the war was won.

Brady   Washington

Among the many puzzles about Grant is where he learned that simple lesson about war, which eluded and continues to elude so many generals, and what made this unassuming, deceptively quiet, shabbily dressed man, with a long history of personal failure and disappointment, turn almost overnight into a formidable commander of men.

He, who had failed at almost everything he tried, succeeded quite suddenly as a general, infused with unmistakable self-confidence and unshaken by the noise, carnage, and confusion of battle. People—particularly his old army colleagues on both sides of the war, not to mention many of his fellow citizens of Galena, Illinois—wondered where the "new" Grant had come from, but the truth is that the new Grant was always present in the old one.

You just had to look carefully, and most people hadn't bothered.

CHAPTER

2

G rant's virtues—his reserve, his quiet determination, his courage in the face of adversity—were all present in the shy, awkward, withdrawn child who seemed unable to please his father and toward whom his mother showed an indifference that was remarked on even at the very beginning of his life.

In a place—a small town on the Ohio River, where his bustling, self-important, and ambitious father, Jesse Grant, ran the tannery—and at a time—1822—when the high rate of infant mortality must have made many women feel that getting too attached to a baby was tempting fate, Hannah Grant's apparent lack of interest in her own son is still curious, and it appears always to have puzzled Grant. Even allowing for the fact that people on or near the frontier didn't fuss about babies and small children as they do today—largely an emotional self-protective mechanism—her detachment is hard to explain, and her attitude actually became stronger as the boy grew older.

It took Hannah six weeks to name her firstborn, which was certainly unusual, and it appears to have been by her wishes that he was named Ulysses, a romantic and, as it turned out, inappropriate name, since as an adult Grant would be quite the reverse of the sly fox of Homer's poem, who outwitted so many stronger warriors and whose cunning was legendary. The hunchbacked Duke of Gloucester, before he takes the throne, congratulates himself (in Shakespeare's words) on being able "to deceive as slyly as Ulysses could," but sly deception would never be one of Ulysses Grant's strengths—he was guileless, straightforward, and incapable of deceit, "naïve as a baby," as Mark Twain put it.

Nobody seems to know why Hannah, a woman of firm religious belief (of the Methodist persuasion), should have been attracted to a name out of the Greek classics—there are stories that when the Grants were unable to agree on a name for their son, they sat down with their friends and relations and asked everyone at the table to write a name on a slip of paper, fold the slip, and put it in a bowl, and "Ulysses" was written on the one Mrs. Grant pulled out (perhaps her mother's). This seems unlikely—to Hannah Grant the whole procedure would have seemed a lot like gambling, and Methodists were as strongly against gambling as they were against drinking—but whatever the reason, she waited six weeks before naming the child and then picked a very odd name indeed. Ulysses' father prefaced it with the name "Hiram," but his mother stuck stubbornly to Ulysses or "Lyss" to the end of her life, and whatever his feelings on the subject, Jesse Grant eventually went along with it.

(The taste for classical names was something of a fad at the time. In much the same way that names like Tara, Bambi, and Tiffany have supplanted Elizabeth, Susan, and Ann in our own day, American Protestants, as they moved farther away from the Puritan heartland of New England, began to feel free to reject names based on the New Testament [John, Matthew, Mark, and so on], or those based on the Old Testament [Isaac, Abraham, Israel, Noah, and the like], in favor of names that had a more "classical" and less religious ring to them, such as Ulysses. Whether it was Hannah or her mother who chose it, Ulysses, with its classical and pagan connections, is hardly a name that Cotton Mather would have condoned for an infant 150 years earlier in Massachusetts.)

In the nineteenth century, presidential candidates liked to boast that

Birthplace of
Ulysses S. Grant

they had been "born in a log cabin," and some were, of course, but Grant was not among them. His birthplace in Point Pleasant, Ohio, was a well-situated farmhouse with a view of the Ohio River, not a log cabin in the woods. Jesse Grant had his failings—many of which were to plague his son Ulysses once he had become a great and famous man—but he was a good provider, by the standards of the day, and not a rude pioneer but a skilled craftsman determined to make his way up in the world as fast as possible. The Grants could—and did—trace their ancestry in America back to 1630, when Matthew and Priscilla Grant came over from England on the *Mary and John*, and claimed, possibly without justification—the matter is open to doubt—that Noah Grant, Jesse's father, had fought as a captain of the militia at Lexington and Concord.

While the Grants did not "come over on the *Mayflower*," they still came over early enough for the family to maintain a strong pride in its roots—a fact that is important to bear in mind. The Grants did not rise to great wealth in the new world, and they moved restlessly westward from generation to generation in search of it, to places where the concept of "landed gentry" was unknown, but their family pride was quite as strong as that of the Lees of Virginia. Modern biographers and historians relish the contrast between the seedy-looking Grant, who was "born on the frontier," and the aristocratic Virginian Lee, but they overlook the fact that Grant considered himself to be every bit Lee's social equal: No child of Jesse Grant's could have thought otherwise.

Grant was not a snob (although later in life he would relish the applause of crowds and the company of crowned heads), but he would never have stooped to play the country bumpkin, as Lincoln did so successfully, and much as he would dislike West Point, he never forgot that he had been there, and expected, in his quiet but firm way, to be treated like an officer and a gentleman. People might see him as an "ordinary man" who had— late in life, and improbably—made good, and many contemporary writers have in fact seen in his career the triumph of the "ordinary man" and taken that as the explanation for his two terms in the White House and the remarkable veneration in which he was held, but there is no indication that Grant ever thought himself as ordinary at all, or that the Grant family had ever considered themselves to be in the least ordinary.

The Grants may not have thought themselves *better* than anyone, but they certainly thought themselves as *good* as anyone—a very American attitude. Jesse Grant pulled himself up by his own bootstraps (as the saying went) to become a small entrepreneur in the leather business, and by the time Ulysses was one year old his father had moved the family to Georgetown, in the adjoining county, hardly a metropolis but offering a better scope for business.

Grant's view of his own childhood takes up only seven of the more than twelve hundred pages of his memoirs, and he scarcely mentions Hannah in them at all, giving no hint of her feelings toward him or his toward her. Her reserve was such as to make some of Grant's biographers speculate that she may have been retarded, but this seems unlikely, not only because it is hard to imagine that Jesse Grant, a talkative, ambitious busybody, would marry anybody retarded, but also because on the few occasions when Hannah is recorded as having said something, it is usually sharp, pithy, and to the point.

To those familiar with what is now called "the Midwestern character" (it was "Western" back then in the early nineteenth century, when Ohio and Illinois were still close to the frontier), Hannah's silence, strong religious faith, and reluctance to explore her own emotions or talk to strangers would not seem unfamiliar or strange. There are still plenty of women out there today who don't wear their heart on their sleeve and don't gush over or about their children. Much is made of the fact that when Grant went back to see his mother after the war, she merely said, "Well, Ulysses, you've become a great man now," and went back inside to her chores, but much the same stories are told about Ike's mother and Harry Truman's, and it need not necessarily mean that Hannah was not pleased by her son's success. Perhaps what mattered most to Hannah Grant was that her son should not get "a swollen head" merely because he was the victorious commander of the U.S. Army, but if that was the case, she need have had no fears—Ulysses was the last person in the world to let success go to his head. His childhood might have been specifically designed to prevent it.

Descriptions of Grant's childhood tend to sound a little like pages from *Huckleberry Finn*, but this is partly because Grant did not dwell on it much, so biographers have been left to invent most of it, in the manner of Parson

Weems reinventing George Washington's childhood as an improving tale. There does not seem to have been any conflict between Ulysses and his siblings (he had two younger brothers and three younger sisters), and there is no evidence that he was particularly unhappy—though of course in those days children weren't *expected* to be happy, nor was life organized to produce happiness for them. A much-told story about Grant relates how, when he was an infant, he crawled out into the street and came to a stop between the hooves of a team of horses that was tethered outside. Terrified neighbors ran to inform Mrs. Grant of the danger her son was in, but to their surprise she did not run out to rescue him, figuring fatalistically perhaps that if Ulysses could get himself into that dangerous position, he could also get himself out of it. Or it may be that Hannah Grant had already learned one of the most remarkable things about her son—that he had a natural empathy for horses, a gift for calming them that was to last all his life. Ulysses was not afraid of horses, and they were not afraid of him, and from a very early age he gained a statewide reputation as an early-nineteenth-century version of "the Horse Whisperer," a talent he never lost.

We do not know how Grant went about "gentling" difficult and fractious horses, and he may not have known himself. He spoke to them softly and calmly, he stroked them, he never resorted to punishment with the whip—but the important thing was that somehow the horses sensed that Grant was their friend, and they trusted him. Had he been able to achieve the same effect with politicians and financiers, his presidency might have been more successful.

There has been a tendency to take Grant's special feel for horses as a matter of small importance, or to claim that it was a skill shared by many people who grew up on a farm, but that is a mistake. Gentling and calming horses was a rare and valuable skill in the days when the horse was practically the only means of transportation, and the fact that people brought their horses to the young Grant from miles away must have made him something of a minor celebrity. We are told that even as a boy of ten he could ride horses nobody else could, and gentle horses everybody else had given up on—valuable accomplishments in an age when a farm horse represented a substantial investment.

Stories of Grant's horsemanship—it was the sole subject in which he would excel at West Point—are legion, but one is worth retelling. Charged with bringing home an unbroken and difficult horse, the boy harnessed it to a buggy, only to have the horse run away with him and nearly take him straight off the edge of a steep cliff or embankment. The horse stopped, trembling and sweating, at the very precipice, and young Grant stepped out of the buggy as quietly as he could so as not to further alarm it. Then, after a moment's reflection, he quickly bound his bandanna around the horse's eyes, having heard somewhere that blind horses seldom run away. Blindfolded, the horse allowed itself to be calmed and then led back to the road. Once Grant resumed his seat in the buggy, the horse, still blind-folded, set off placidly, guided by the reins, and made no further attempt to bolt.

It is evident from this story that Grant not only had an innate sympathy for horses but used his intelligence to outwit them and calm their fears—he did not attempt to subdue horses, he outthought them. Not many adults, let alone boys, would have had the presence of mind to come up with the stratagem of blindfolding a runaway horse, or the courage to get back into the buggy and set off on a long trip with a horse that had just confirmed its reputation of being dangerous.

Grant was not outstanding at school, even in the undemanding "sub-scription" school at Georgetown, and though he was a hard worker on the farm Jesse soon bought, there was nothing unusual about that at a time when young boys were *expected* to work hard on a farm—indeed, one of the reasons people wanted large families was to provide a good source of obedient young workers. The young Grant was remarkable, though not necessarily admired, for his refusal to kill animals. He not only disliked all forms of hunting, an aversion that he maintained all his life, but also avoided eating meat whenever he could, and would only touch it if it was burned to a crisp—the sight of blood on his plate turned his stomach. Early on he developed a pronounced dislike for swearing and for smutty stories, and in later life would never allow either to take place in his presence, an unusual characteristic in an army officer.

It does not come as a surprise that the only occasion during the entire Civil War when Grant is recorded as having lost his temper was in Virginia, in late May 1864. He came across a teamster on the road, whipping a fractious horse about the head and face. After what was described as "an explosion of anger," Grant ordered the offender tied to a post for several hours, then rode off down the road to launch the Battle of Cold Harbor, one of the bloodiest frontal battles of the war. Grant was clearly among the most unusual of men—one who could not bear to see bloody meat on his plate

General Grant & his War Horse.

Grant and his favorite horse, Cincinnati, during the Civil War

or an animal killed or a horse whipped, but who could send men into a battle that lasted almost a week and in which the last assault, by three Union corps, was repulsed with the loss of more than seven thousand men in less than half an hour. The wounded lay where they had fallen, in what was called "a slaughter pen," for almost a week in the sweltering sun, picked off by Confederate sharpshooters or dying of thirst, before Grant could bring himself to request a truce to remove them. Though he later reflected in his memoirs, "I have always regretted that the last assault at Cold Harbor was made," and though his conduct of the battle was by no means typical of Grant's generalship, it is worth noting that it was the plight of a horse that drew his anger at Cold Harbor, not the plight of the men.

As a boy he seems to have led a lonely life. His father, Jesse, was building up his business and beginning to seek a political career, or at least to become a citizen of importance, while his mother, Hannah, closed herself off from him. It is perhaps because of this that Ulysses relished the company of horses, and felt with them something he missed in his home life. Among the other children of his age in Georgetown, his peculiar first name was habitually turned into "Useless" Grant, and the combination of a strange name, a certain shy awkwardness, and a degree of prudery unusual among young boys then (or indeed at any time) must have made him a natural victim of taunts and bullying. He seems also to have been a sensitive and easily wounded boy, though determined to hide the fact as much as he could. Certainly he was never seen to cry as a boy, or later when he was grown up, but all photographs of him show a certain melancholy in his expression, which those who were closest to him in later life— General Sherman, for instance—recognized: Grant looked like somebody who *would* have cried if he could.

Photographs of Jesse and Hannah, however, make it clear that tears were not an option for them, and therefore probably not for any child who wanted their approval, which Ulysses most certainly did. He learned stoicism early, though at a cost.

At school the one subject he seems to have excelled at was arithmetic, but most of his time was not spent in studies but in working on the farm, particularly with the horses, with which he could perform miracles. Though gratifying to Jesse, it was not enough to satisfy him. His firstborn son, he felt strongly, should follow him into his tannery business, learn the trade, and make something of himself.

But if there was one trade Ulysses knew he didn't want to follow, it was tanning leather. The tannery was next to the house, with its noxious smells of rendered fat and dried blood, and from his room he could hear the lowing of the frightened old cattle that were penned up outside waiting to be slaughtered, and their screams as they were killed.

Tanning began—it was the most important step—with removing the hide from the animal's body, scraping all the fat and blood off the inside of it, then turning it over and scraping off the hair. For a young man who couldn't bear to see animals killed and who from a very young age wouldn't eat meat unless it was burned beyond recognition, this was not an apprenticeship he could have welcomed. It is to Jesse's credit that while Ulysses' doubts about entering the tannery business may have dismayed him, he knew a lost cause when he saw one. On the grounds that an education might do Ulysses some good—it was that or let him become a farm worker—Jesse took the unusual step of writing to his congressman to propose Ulysses for West Point (without bothering to inform Ulysses). What Hannah thought of it we do not know, though she might have echoed Wellington's mother, who said of him as a child, when it was decided he should be a soldier, "So my poor Arthur is fit for nothing but food for powder."

His appointment to West Point was unusual in a good many ways, the most important being that Jesse, in his role as a politically ambitious busy-body, had alienated Thomas L. Hamer, the congressman from his district. Hamer was a Democrat, while Jesse Grant was a Whig, and given to intemperate and outspoken political arguments, during the course of which he had said any number of things that offended Hamer when he heard about them. Nevertheless Jesse swallowed his pride and wrote to Hamer; and Hamer, perhaps out of good nature, or more likely because he thought it might shut Jesse up, agreed to give the vacant appointment in his control to young Ulysses Grant.

At this point in Grant's young life (he was sixteen) his legal name was Hiram Ulysses Grant, but Representative Hamer could not be expected to know that, since everyone always referred to the boy as Ulysses. Hamer knew that Ulysses had a middle name and, taking a wild guess, made the assumption that it was probably Simpson, after Hannah's family. He wrote to the War Department to inform them that his choice for the vacancy was Ulysses Simpson Grant. Thus, accidentally, Grant's name would be recorded by the War Department and at West Point as U. S. Grant.[1]

W est Point, when Grant arrived there in May 1839, was not then the vast institution it is now, of course, and indeed the U.S. Army at the time was itself small and inbred. Many in the United States still regarded the whole idea of a professional army, however small (and of West Point itself), with deep suspicion. America was a democracy—the creation of a military elite seemed profoundly undemocratic. Quite apart from that, there was the question of what purpose the army served. The only enemy the United States had fought in the past was Great Britain, but relationships with the former mother country were becoming increasingly cordial, so apart from garrisoning a few forlorn forts against the Indians on the frontier, there was not much for the army to do. What is more, the legend of a "citizen army"—based on the experience of Concord, Lexington, and Bunker Hill—played a large part in the country's national self-image. Great Britain and the European monarchies might have strutting "regulars" and an aristocratic officer corps, but despite the experience of the Revolutionary War and the War of 1812—both of which had eventually been won by trained regulars, not the militia—the ideal of the Minute Man leaving his farm with his rifle over his shoulder to fight the Redcoats, and voting to select his own officers, was a potent, mythic part of the national consciousness.

The antithesis of this point of view was represented by Gen. Winfield Scott, a hero of the War of 1812, who commanded the army, and was known, though not to his face, as "Old Fuss and Feathers." General Scott had grown so corpulent that he could no longer mount a horse, and the magnificence of his uniforms and his plumed hat explains his nickname; but he still commanded great respect, and his authority in military matters was unchallenged. In some ways Scott reminds one of Lord Raglan, in Great Britain, who had been the Duke of Wellington's devoted military secretary (and who lost an arm at Waterloo), then went on to command the British army. Like Scott, Raglan (after whom the Raglan sleeve is named) was both courageous and resolutely determined to stand in the way of change. It was Raglan's habit, when any proposal for change in the army was brought up, to say, "Let us consider what the great Duke of Wellington would do," and then to do nothing. So firmly rooted in the past was Raglan that even when he commanded the British army in the Crimea against Russia, with France as an ally, he was nevertheless in the habit of automatically referring to the enemy as "the French."

Not even Scott, however, with his ponderous bulk, magnificent uniforms, and overpowering personality, could make the profession of arms respectable or desirable in the United States. At the time, people became soldiers because they had failed at everything else in life. As for West

Point, it was virtually the only way to get a college education of sorts at government expense; and for many of those who went there, a vast social step upward.

Grant went there without enthusiasm or argument—no doubt it sounded a better bet than the tannery—and his first act was to accept the change of his name without putting up a fuss about it. It was mildly embarrassing to have his first initials become U.S., but not nearly as bad as having those on his trunk be "H.U.G." Very shortly he was called "Uncle Sam," and as a result he soon became known to most of his fellow cadets as "Sam Grant." After being taunted as "Useless" in school, this development must have come as a relief.[2]

Grant did not do well at West Point—although his interest in mathematics was noted with approval, and not only was his horsemanship much admired, but he set a record height for jumping a horse that had remained unbroken for twenty-five years. His dress, deportment, and appearance were slovenly by West Point standards; he seemed to have no interest in girls or dancing or any form of social life; and his interest in military tactics was negligible. Neither then nor later did he read, study, or even own any of the great books on tactics, which perhaps merely confirms Napoleon's remark that "in war, as in prostitution, the amateur is often better than the professional."

Not surprisingly Grant was put in the "awkward squad," composed of young men who were no good at drill, and stayed there for an uncommonly long time, a misfit in the eyes of most of his fellow cadets—awkward, lonely, unmilitary in appearance and bearing, and happy only in the riding ring. Although he grew to five feet eight inches, not a bad height for the mid–nineteenth century, he was only five feet two when he arrived at West Point, and must therefore also have seemed more a child than a young man, despite his great strength. Although his classmates included James Longstreet, William Rosecrans, William Hardee, John Pope, Richard

Ewell, and Buckner, all of whom went on to become generals on one side or the other in the Civil War, only Buckner seemed to remember him later on (though it did him little good when he sought surrender terms from Grant at Fort Donelson). Longstreet hardly remembered Grant at all, despite three years together at West Point. He seems to have been about as invisible as a cadet can be. In later life, though he professed a great respect for West Point, he recalled, "The most trying days of my life were those I spent there, and I never recall them with pleasure."

Even his graduation caused him no pleasure. Given his love of horses, he had hoped for appointment to a cavalry regiment, but since there were no vacancies he was obliged to settle for an infantry regiment instead. His one consolation was that in those days infantry officers usually rode, rather than marching alongside the soldiers and noncommissioned officers, so he would at least have a horse to keep him busy.

CHAPTER

3

In England there was a vast social gulf between cavalry and infantry regiments (with the exception of the regiments of the Foot Guards), but that was not the case in the United States. Those cadets who graduated at the top of their class from West Point were appointed to the engineers (like Robert E. Lee) or to the artillery, both branches in which brains were thought to be in demand.

It cannot but have been a disappointment for a shy young second lieutenant who had hoped to serve in the cavalry to arrive at Jefferson Barracks, a few miles outside St. Louis, Missouri, to join the Fourth Infantry in 1843. Having failed to get into the cavalry, Grant had applied to be a teacher of mathematics at West Point, but this too was not to be. He was stuck in the infantry and would have to make the best of it, and make the best of Missouri as well.

Grant was not then nor later in life a man who was fussy about his surroundings, but an army post in those days would have been a lonely place for a youngster, and the endless parades, drills, and fussy inspections of the infantry cannot have done much to cheer him up.

His fellow officers played cards, drank, smoked, and idled the day away, and spent as much time as they could off post in nearby St. Louis, attending dances and trying to meet young women—none of them pursuits of much interest to Grant, who had never learned how to dance. After seven long months the Fourth Infantry was ordered down the Mississippi River to a temporary posting in western Louisiana, on the Texas border—even less promising country, and with even less to do for a second lieutenant who loved horses.

At some point Grant became friendly with a big, bluff, cheerful young officer who had been in his class at West Point, Frederick T. Dent, and on returning to Jefferson Barracks, Dent invited Grant to his home, a farm near St. Louis. The Dents were a large family, on the borderline of being "gentry," and Southern in their sympathies, their origins, and their traditions. Frederick's father, "Colonel" Dent, was a slave owner on a small scale, affable and reasonably prosperous, but White Haven, though comfortable enough, was a simple farmhouse—a far cry from the great antebellum mansions of the Deep South—and later attempts by Mrs. Grant to portray the Dents as Southern oligarchs or White Haven as Tara, in the masterful phrase of William S. McFeely in his 1981 biography of Grant, were largely spurious.[1]

The Dents had made their way from Maryland to Missouri via Pittsburgh, and both there and in St. Louis, Colonel Dent had engaged rather languidly in "trade" to make the money to buy the farm, where he spent most of his time reading books and pontificating on politics. Laziness would seem to have been his besetting sin, rather than slave owning.

Mrs. Dent, who had genteel social ambitions and a flair for self-dramatization worthy of a mother in a Tennessee Williams play, is said to have deeply resented being stuck on a farm outside St. Louis rather than being at the center of that city's social life, where she felt she belonged. The Dents had six children, four boys and two girls: Ellen, usually called Nellie, and Julia.

Making allowances for the differences between North and South, the Dents were not that much more elevated on the socioeconomic scale than were the Grants in Ohio, though Mrs. Dent was certainly a good deal more talkative and fashion conscious than the reclusive Hannah Grant,

Grant as a lieutenant

and Colonel Dent, though shrewd enough, was the very opposite of the kind of hard-edged, self-made, bustling Yankee businessman that Jesse Grant was. One can easily imagine, however, the effect that the lively Dents must have had on the lonely Ulysses Grant, and how much it must have meant to him to be accepted into the family.

Apparently the first of the Dent sisters that he met was Nellie, but shortly afterward he and Julia met, and there took place what the French call *un coup de foudre*—love at first sight—at least on Julia's part. They were soon spending many hours riding together—it is unclear whether Julia was an enthusiastic horsewoman or simply guessed it was the best way of engaging Ulysses' interest—and before long, despite his shyness and awkwardness, they reached an "understanding." Grant had finally found somebody who brought him out of his lonely and self-imposed isolation, who loved and admired him, and with whom he could talk. As for Julia, she had found her *beau idéal*. Ulysses Grant was good-looking, morally serious, and completely, if inarticulately, devoted to her. If ever two people qualified for the term "soul mates" they were Julia and Ulysses. For the rest of his days his marriage to Julia would be at the center of his life, and he would be, even after his death, the center of hers. Perhaps only the marriage of Queen Victoria and Prince Albert was as close and as satisfying to both partners—certainly the Grants would have one of the great marriages of the nineteenth century.

Of course they had to get there first. Grant had few prospects—a second lieutenant's pay was exiguous, and in peacetime, promotion was glacially slow—while Julia was, to put it kindly, "plain," as even her nearest and dearest in the Dent family were obliged to admit. Indeed, "plain" seems like a generous description of Julia Dent. A photograph of her taken as a young woman, at about the time that Grant was courting her (or, to be more accurate, when she was courting him), reveals a lumpy nose, a strong chin, and what appears to be a pronounced squint in one eye, or perhaps, as McFeely suggests, strabismus, a weakening of the eye muscles combined with a squint (some people unkindly described her as wall-eyed), hair pulled back unflatteringly tight, and a compact, dumpy figure. The fashions of the times apparently do nothing to help her, and her expression in the photograph is severe, impatient, and unwelcoming. Although she was to come to think of herself as a Southern belle, a kind of border-state Scarlett O'Hara, Julia was by far the plainest member of the Dent family, and even the colored servants (slaves, of course) seem to have told her so.

Neither the Dents nor the Grants were much pleased by the prospect of this union. Even allowing for Julia's plainness, her father, Colonel Dent, no doubt hoped for something better for his daughter than a second lieutenant whose father was a moderately successful leather tanner in Ohio; and as for Jesse Grant, he thought his son was too young to marry—Ulysses was twenty-two and Julia seventeen when they met—and was anything but pleased at the prospect of a daughter-in-law whose parents were slave-owning Southerners. It appears, however, that Grant screwed up his determination, perhaps for the first and most significant time, and his determination was more than matched by Julia's—throughout their lives, her willpower, ambition, and determination would far exceed his. In any event, their devotion to each other, as in good novels, was so strong and self-evident as to overcome all obstacles and objections.

The British army had a saying that "A lieutenant must not marry, a captain may marry, a major must marry," a rule that remained true until well into the twentieth century, but in the U.S. Army in the nineteenth century, lieutenants married young, and it was generally considered to be a good thing. Given the godforsaken outposts in which army units were stationed, mostly on the frontier, in the middle of nowhere, a wife and children had a steadying effect on young men who might otherwise have taken to drink, whoring, or gambling to fill up the time. Grant would eventually fall prey to one of these vices himself, but it is worth noting that when he became engaged to Julia he was abstemious, and that later on he usually drank when he was separated from her or, as in Galena, when he was plunged so deep into misery, failure, and debt that not even she could talk him out of it.

But that was in the future. The young people agreed, no doubt reluctantly, to a long engagement (it would last four years), but it must have been clear to everybody that however lengthy the engagement, nothing would change their minds about each other.

There is a wonderful story—told in numerous versions—that when Grant rode out to White Haven from Jefferson Barracks to ask for Julia's hand, he found a stream in full flood and was unable to ford it. Instead of turning back, however, he plunged in, swam his horse through a raging torrent, and had to borrow dry civilian clothes when he arrived at the Dents' home. This incident is notable not only because it underlines Grant's fearless horsemanship and his determination, but also because it is the first known example of a very important peculiarity of his character: Grant had an extreme, almost phobic dislike of turning back and retracing his steps. If he set out for somewhere, he would *get* there somehow, whatever the difficulties that lay in his way. This idiosyncrasy would turn out to be one of the factors that made him a formidable general. Grant would always, always press on—turning back was not an option for him.

The years of their engagement were those of a gathering storm—and here it is necessary to pause briefly and describe the political situation of the United States in the 1840s, as it was to affect Ulysses and Julia. In 1836 Texas, then largely populated by white Americans, had declared its independence of Mexico, and after a short and bloody campaign, seceded from Mexico and became an independent state. The Republic of Texas was soon recognized by the United States but not by Mexico, and American business interests moved quickly to finance the infant republic, while the administration of President Andrew Jackson surreptitiously provided the Texans with arms and volunteers.

Demands for the annexation of Texas as a state increased—the loans made to the republic would be more secure if it became part of the United States, so Wall Street was in favor of annexation; but, more important, if Texas came into the Union, it would come in as a slave state—or perhaps more than one slave state, for it was so big that there was talk of carving it into as many as four entities. Four states would have added eight pro-slavery senators to the Southern bloc in the U.S. Senate, giving the South a decisive advantage over the Northern states on the highly charged question of expanding slavery in the West, and securing the survival of the "peculiar institution," as it was referred to by Southerners.

The skeleton of slavery had been rattling its bones in the closet of American politics ever since the Declaration of Independence—indeed the

Declaration itself could never have been signed had not Jefferson found a way of evading the issue—and by the time Ulysses Grant went to West Point it was clear enough that while most people in the North did not condone slavery, they were prepared to live with it, if necessary, provided it was not expanded into the new territories to the West, or farther south.

Southerners saw the matter differently, of course—slavery was legal, however uncomfortable it might make people in Massachusetts or New York, and the South was entitled to expand it into the new territories and farther south into Mexico and the Caribbean if it could. The Missouri Compromise of 1820 had banned slavery from all territory west of the Mississippi River and north of a line drawn westward from the southern border of Missouri, but its constitutionality was under continuous challenge. In any event, the possible annexation of Texas was perceived as a threat by Northerners, and by Southerners as an opportunity to break out of what were increasingly seen as artificial restraints against the spread of slavery.

In the North only a small minority argued for abolition, while in the South an equally small minority advocated the unrestrained growth of a slave empire, but as is so often the case, the extremists on both sides soon began to dominate, then to define the argument. The notion that the Negro might be freed and made the equal of the white man was hardly more popular in the North than in the South, and what was to be done with the slaves in the event that slavery could be ended (if possible by gradual, peaceful means, with the slave owners compensated) remained a vexatious if academic question in American politics. The idea of repatriating the slaves to Africa was eventually responsible for the creation of Liberia, and the somewhat more practical idea of settling the slaves in a state or territory of their own was often discussed, but without much conviction or energy.

The fight over the annexation of Texas brought the slavery issue once again into sharp focus as the great national political divide, to the discomfort of many, but the matter was sealed when the Texans shrewdly set in motion negotiations in London to make the Republic of Texas part of the British Empire. Even staunch nonannexationists were startled and dismayed at the prospect of the British Empire reappearing on North American soil. This threat was one of the many factors that led to proannexationist James K. Polk's victory in the presidential election of 1844, and to the subsequent annexation of Texas (which succeeded only by the skin of its teeth). Polk and the Southerners—not to speak of the Texans themselves, once they had joined the Union—had a greater ambition, however, which was to seize as much Mexican territory as they could, at least everything north of the Rio Grande. The unsettled dispute over the southern border of Texas, which had festered from the very beginning of the Texas Republic as a sore point between the Texans and Mexico, seemed tailor-made as a cause for war, if only the Mexicans could be provoked into beginning it. The Mexicans claimed that their border with Texas was on the Nueces River, while the Texans (and now the United States) argued that it was on the Rio Grande—a difference of about 120 miles. It was not much as a cause for war, but it was enough. Polk moved U.S. forces into the disputed region, calculating that their presence there would sooner or later provoke Mexico to fight.

The maneuverings that were to lead to the Mexican War were the background against which Ulysses and Julia's engagement took place, meaning that during a great part of that time he was absent, as the Fourth Infantry was moved first to Nachitoches for a year, on the western edge of Louisiana, close to Texas, and then, via New Orleans, to Corpus Christi, Texas, a small part of a military show that was intended to overbear the Mexicans, and impress them with the might and the serious intentions of the United States. Grant was an unenthusiastic bit player in this drama—he was no friend to slavery, he disliked the idea of using the army to provoke the

Mexicans into a war they would lose, and he had no great desire to fight Mexicans or anybody else. On top of which duty kept him separated from Julia, and from pressing Colonel Dent to agree to an earlier marriage.

As a result he wrote—long, detailed letters, full of intelligent observations and interesting detail, in which his passion for Julia occasionally surfaces quite movingly. These are not the letters of an ordinary second lieutenant. During his days in West Point, Grant's superiors had complained that he wasted his time reading "romantic novels" (improbable as that might seem in a young man as dour as Grant), but if that was the case it did more for his style as a writer than reading Jomini's classic text on tactics would have done. Like the young Winston Churchill, also a failure at school and military college, Grant learned how to master the English sentence. His spelling left much to be desired, but his prose is direct, clear, and never ambiguous, as it was to be for the rest of his life, and his letters certainly served their purpose in keeping Julia's attentions directed toward him and lobbying her father (unsuccessfully) to let them marry sooner. They also make clear that Grant, however much he missed his Julia, was stimulated by the unfamiliar countryside, and his descriptions of life in Texas and Mexico, as well as life in the camp, are lively, detailed, and thoughtful—just the thing to keep his fiancée, back in St. Louis, amused and interested.

It is interesting to note, for example, that in order to relieve the tedium of waiting in Corpus Christi, then a sleepy Mexican village, for the Mexican government to lose patience and go to war, the junior officers organized an amateur theatrical company. One of the productions they put on was *Othello*, in which Ulysses Grant, improbably, was persuaded to play Desdemona. James Longstreet (the future Confederate general) also played in the company, and complained that Grant's portrayal of Desdemona was something less than convincing, and that he had to be replaced by a professional actress sent from New Orleans, but the sight of the future victor of

Shiloh and Vicksburg in the costume of a young woman of sixteenth-century Venice must have been memorable indeed—a number of people who were present at Appomattox twenty years later certainly still remembered it vividly.[2]

More typically, struck by the huge herds of wild horses in the area, Grant purchased a large number of them at three dollars a head, hoping to sell them for twice that, only to lose his investment when they all ran away—a warning sign of Grant's lifelong inability to bring even the simplest of commercial transactions to a profitable conclusion.

In the meantime the army had advanced beyond the Nueces, and when that did not persuade the Mexicans to fight, continued on, at a lethargic pace even for the day, toward the Rio Grande. In command of the army was Gen. Zachary Taylor, whose nickname, "Old Rough and Ready," might have been chosen to emphasize the contrast between himself and "Old Fuss and Feathers," General Scott. Zachary Taylor wore plain, dusty civilian clothes instead of a uniform, unpolished boots, and a slouch hat, and was in the habit of sitting sideways on his horse to observe the movement of his troops, with both legs hanging down over one side, as if he were lounging in an easy chair. It may be that Grant's first glimpse of Taylor imprinted itself on his mind—or at any rate imprinted on it for future reference the notion that a general need not necessarily be a military fashion plate to succeed in battle.

Taylor's strategy was to push toward the nearest big Mexican town—Matamoros, about 150 miles from Corpus Christi—a process that would take months, given the arid, uninhabited nature of the countryside, the paucity of wells, drinkable river water, and fodder, and the fact that the army was moving at the pace of the mules and oxen that provided its transport. Eventually, however, Taylor got his army across the disputed territory and proceeded to build a small fort across the Rio Grande from Matamoras, a challenge which the Mexicans could hardly refuse, with the result that in April 1846 the administration, Wall Street, the Texans, and the South finally got the war they had been looking for.

Grant was not overjoyed at the prospect—like General Taylor, he did not believe this was a just war, and he rather liked the Mexicans—but on May 8, at Palo Alto, he received his baptism of fire as the three thousand men of Taylor's army, having finally encountered the Mexican army, formed a line of battle and advanced toward the considerably larger forces of the enemy. "I thought what a fearful responsibility General Taylor must feel," Grant wrote later, "commanding such a host and so far away from friends."

During the exchange of artillery fire that decided the battle—Taylor was equipped with more modern, longer-range artillery than the Mexicans, which fired exploding shells rather than solid balls—Grant was in the thick of things. "One canon [*sic*] ball passed through our ranks, not far from me. It took off the head of an enlisted man, and the under jaw of Captain Page of my regiment, while the splinters of the musket of the killed soldier, and his brains and bones, knocked down two or three others, including one officer, Lieutenant Wallen." Grant's matter-of-fact prose does not disguise the horror of warfare, then or now.

On the ninth Grant fought in another battle, at Resaca, in which he took temporary command of a company, captured a wounded Mexican colonel, and observed that "the battle of Resaca de la Palma would have been won, just as it was, had I not been there." Tolstoy could not have put it better. Nevertheless, reading between the lines, it is possible to discern that Grant had demonstrated, if nothing else, a keen power of observation, a capacity for command, no tendency to panic or flinch under fire, and a strong stomach for the awful scenes of combat—in short, that he had the makings of a real soldier.

During the lengthy time that the army spent at Matamoras, Grant met many of the officers who would be his opponents or his fellow Union generals in the Civil War, and his sharp memory would pay dividends later on, for he could often guess what they would do in command based on how they had behaved in Mexico—hence his instinctive judgment that Buckner would cave under pressure at Fort Donelson. He served with such future Confederate generals as Lee, Joseph E. Johnston, and Albert Sidney Johnston (no relation), and later remarked in his memoirs, "My appreciation of my enemies was certainly affected by this knowledge. The natural disposition of most people is to clothe a commander of a large army whom they do not know, with almost superhuman abilities. A large part of the National army, for instance, and most of the press of the country, clothed General Lee with just such qualities, but I had known him personally, *and knew that he was mortal* [italics added]."

The problem of overestimating or even hero-worshipping successful enemy commanders in time of war was not, of course, confined to nineteenth-century America. In World War II "the Rommel factor," much resembling the universal admiration for Lee, overcame the British public and most British generals until Gen. Sir Bernard Law Montgomery (as he was then) finally beat Field Marshal Erwin Rommel at El Alamein and put an end to Rommel's reputation for invincibility and battlefield omniscience. Apparently undiminished by defeat, however, Rommel's legend, like Lee's, continues to impress historians and biographers.

Among the officers Grant met, surprisingly, was none other than Congressman Hamer, who had yielded to Jesse Grant's request to get his son into West Point and was now a major of the Ohio volunteers, waiting to be appointed a brigadier general—an object lesson for Grant in the uses of political influence and in the ease with which amateur soldiers climbed the ladder of promotion in wartime, as opposed to professionals.

Eventually the army, now reinforced to 6,500 men, lurched through the Sierra Madre mountains to threaten Monterrey, the last major town on the long road to Mexico City, defended by a garrison of more than ten thousand. After a short siege Taylor attacked the city, and Grant was caught up in the street fighting that followed, distinguishing himself by volunteering to ride back through the streets under a hail of rifle fire to ask for more ammunition to be sent up. He rode at a full gallop, Indian style, clinging to the side of his horse to shield himself from the enemy's fire, with one foot cocked over the cantle of the saddle and an arm around the horse's neck—the kind of thing Kevin Costner (or his stuntman) might do in a movie today (not unlike the scene at the beginning of *Dances with Wolves*), but Grant did in real life in Monterrey, with real bullets whizzing around him and his horse's hooves skittering on cobblestones that were, in some places, slippery with blood. The feat won Grant a considerable degree of respect.

At one point stopped by American soldiers, he entered a house and found it full of badly wounded Americans, including two he knew, a captain with a bad head wound and a lieutenant "whose bowels protruded from his wound." He promised to send help, then got back on his horse to resume his run, but in the confusion of battle the wounded Americans "fell into the hands of the enemy during the night, and died."

Here, in his usual clipped, unemotional prose, is another perfect portrait of the horrors of war, a scene (and an outcome) worthy of Goya. By the next day Monterrey had been taken, and Grant's pity was aroused by the sight of the Mexican prisoners of war, particularly the cavalry "on miserable little half-starved horses that did not look as if they could carry their riders out of town."

Few other officers would have been equally moved by the distressing sight of enemy troops taken prisoner and by that of the charnel house of wounded American officers and men, but Grant had that rare quality among professional soldiers, even at the very beginning of his career, of feeling deeply for the wounded and dead of both sides. It was not weakness—it was that he spared himself nothing. Grant saw what happened in war, swallowed his revulsion, pity, and disgust, and went on. He did not, in Yeats's famous phrase, "cast a cold eye on life, on death"; he cast a saddened and mournful one—one has only to look at photographs of him—which nevertheless did not prevent him from doing his job.

In the meantime the war's growing importance was emphasized by the administration's decision to send the aging General in Chief Winfield Scott to take command in Mexico. Scott had no faith in Taylor's attack from the north, and proposed to advance on Vera Cruz, seize it, then march inland on Mexico City. Old Rough and Ready continued his own advance, while his rival, Old Fuss and Feathers, decked out in every feather, sash, and gold decoration the law allowed (as Grant sourly observed) marched slowly on Vera Cruz, both generals having their eyes firmly fixed, in the great American tradition, on the next presidential election.

In the event, Taylor moved faster and fought and won the decisive battle of Buena Vista (February 22–24, 1847) with his army of volunteers against a much larger Mexican force, thus guaranteeing his nomination by the Whig Party and his election as president in 1848.

As for Grant, his regiment was transferred from Taylor's army to Scott's, where Grant found both the slow pace and the insistence on military formality and correct uniforms at all times difficult to bear. He served under Gen. William J. Worth, of whom he commented trenchantly, "Some commanders can move troops so as to get the maximum distance out of them without fatigue, while others can wear them out in a few days without accomplishing so much. General Worth belonged to this latter class."

Grant participated in the siege of Vera Cruz and the Battle of Cerro Gordo (in which Capt. Robert E. Lee played a dashing and glamorous role), after which Grant was appointed quartermaster and sent off with a train of wagons to "procure forage," a position of no glamour but considerable responsibility. If Grant had not bothered to read Napoleon's comment on war—"An army marches on its stomach"—while he was immersed in novels at West Point, he soon got a chance to observe the truth of this maxim in the field as a quartermaster. He also got a chance to compare Taylor and Scott in action, and noted, "Taylor was not a conversationalist, but on paper he could put his meaning so plainly that there could be no mistaking it," a description Grant might as easily have applied to himself.

Scott's army now was in place to advance on Mexico City, and Grant fought at Contreras, Molino del Rey (where he had the quick wit to use an upturned cart to climb onto the roof of a building and overwhelm the Mexicans defending it), and Chapultepec (where his quick action under fire led to the taking of a key portion of the town's defensive line with a few troops he had hastily scratched up). Although he was to write in his memoirs that the Battles of Molino del Rey and Chapultepec were "wholly unnecessary," there is no doubt that he fought courageously in both of them and, in the absence of orders, did not hesitate to use his own bold initiative.

On September 14 American troops finally entered Mexico City, General Scott made his headquarters in the "Halls of the Montezumas," and Ulysses S. Grant was promoted, at last, to first lieutenant, four officers senior to him in his regiment having been killed in a "steamboat explosion," of all things. As always in the regular army, the death of officers senior to oneself, however it occurs, results in the promotion of those below, so Grant was promoted more by the operation of seniority than because of his personal bravery. On the other hand he was a regular officer, he knew the rules, and did not chafe at them.

Whatever his reservations about the Mexican War—and they were many—and however much he sympathized with Mexico over the draconian peace terms that would deprive the country of all its territory north of the Rio Grande and make the United States, at last, a continental power—he was relieved to have done his duty and proved to himself that he was a soldier.

America finally had its "Manifest Destiny"—and with it the now-burning question of whether slavery would be extended to its vast new territories—and Ulysses Grant was anxious to return home to his.

He sweltered on the beach near Vera Cruz while fever raged through the troops, then shipped out to Pascagoula, Mississippi, and immediately obtained a four-month leave of absence.

On August 22, 1848, in St. Louis, he married Julia Dent, perhaps the most important event of his life so far.

CHAPTER

4

G rant had waited a long time to marry Julia, and it is clear enough that while the Dents gave in to the inevitable, they were still not overjoyed. Active military service in Mexico had hardened Grant—he was lean, strong, tanned, very much the picture of a conquering hero—but he was still only an infantry lieutenant, and the son of a bumptious Northern leather tanner at that. Ulysses at last got his Julia, thanks to his patience and persistence, but both Julia and her family made it clear that henceforth it would be his responsibility to measure up to the privilege of marrying her. In a sense this was already something of a Grant family tradition—Jesse Grant had taken Hannah Simpson from the brick house her family lived in (brick houses were a rarity in Point Pleasant, Ohio, at the time), and the implication was that he had "married up." Ulysses, too—at any rate in the eyes of the Dents—had done so, and curiously enough a brick house would play a role in his marriage as well, since Julia yearned for one but was compelled for many years to live in homes she considered beneath her.

That Ulysses and Julia were happy together, physically and emotionally, is crystal clear from their correspondence. No hint of scandal or unfaithfulness would ever touch their lives—Ulysses was the most faithful and devoted of husbands (if not always the most demonstrative) and always would be, while Julia, though more demanding, invariably saw him through rose-colored spectacles. No matter how shabby and down-at-the-heels Grant became—and he would go a long way down before he rose up again—Julia refused to admit it, or possibly even to *see* it. "Captain Grant," as she always called him once he reached that rank, even when he was clerking in his father's leather-goods store, "was always perfection."

In the meantime the young couple's happiness was in the hands of that most unreliable of institutions when it comes to what we now call "human resources"—the peacetime army, which proceeded to do everything possible to make their lives a misery. Grant was posted to Detroit, by no means an enviable posting to begin with in those days, but no sooner had the Grants arrived there than he was ordered, over his protests, to Sackets Harbor, N.Y., a remote outpost on Lake Ontario, where they spent a long, cold winter enjoying their first taste of domestic bliss.

In the spring of 1849, once they had become used to Sackets Harbor, the War Department finally responded to Grant's complaints against being sent there by ordering him back to Detroit, where the Grants settled into a modest house and life among the other junior officers and their wives until Julia returned to St. Louis to have her first child, Frederick Dent Grant (named for her father) at home, while Grant was reassigned again to Sackets Harbor, where mother and child rejoined him in 1851.

In 1852 Grant's regiment was shifted to the Pacific Coast, and although Julia was eager to accompany him, she was pregnant again. It was, in those days, a daunting journey, first by sea to the Isthmus of Panama, then across the mountainous isthmus by mule, in a country where yellow fever and cholera were widespread, and finally the long, rough ocean journey to San Francisco. Many men died of sickness along the way, usually before reaching the Pacific coast of Panama, and no pregnant woman, even one as determined as Julia Grant, would be likely to attempt it.

Grant, it can be perceived, had no friends with influence in the army. He was, besides, ever so slightly under a cloud, having been held responsible for the theft of one thousand dollars while he was a quartermaster in Mexico. Nobody alleged that Grant himself had stolen the money, but the accounts were his responsibility, and he was therefore ordered to repay the sum. Neither his correspondence with the War Department nor Jesse's on his son's behalf was sufficient to straighten out the matter, and even a journey Grant made to Washington at his own expense to explain his case met with failure—partly, no doubt, because accounting was not one of Grant's strengths, and also because he was not particularly forceful or articulate in his own defense.

In any event he sailed from New York City, leaving Julia behind, in the summer of 1852, and after a hazardous and difficult journey eventually reached San Francisco, 150 of the Fourth Infantry party having died of cholera in Panama on the way (about average for the time). Grant's object was to make enough money by small side ventures to bring Julia and the children out to join him, but monotonously, one after another, each attempt failed. A partnership in a general store saw Grant's investment vanish, along with the partner. An attempt to raise hogs failed, as did an attempt to grow potatoes. Whatever Grant tried, bad judgment, bad weather, bad luck got in the way, leaving him poorer than before. It was not from any lack of energy or hard work; Grant simply lacked business sense.

The army hardly kept him busy. He was eventually posted to the Columbia Barracks, at Fort Vancouver, in Washington Territory, as quartermaster— really a store clerk in uniform—and despite the beauties of the countryside, he grew gloomier and lonelier as the months wore on, and as one unsuccessful commercial venture followed another. Even Julia's letters began to express a certain impatience with Ulysses, as she waited in Sackets Harbor with her two sons, Fred and Ulysses Junior (called "Buck" by everybody but his mother), the younger of whom Grant had not so far seen.

It was there, in full view of Mount Hood and the Pacific, that the stories of Grant's drinking began. Let it be said first of all that Grant was never a convivial drunk. He did not haunt barrooms and exchange boozy anecdotes with fellow drinkers. Loneliness, depression, a sense of failure, and the inability to see any improvement in his condition led Grant to drink. He went on solitary binges, alone in his room with a bottle of whiskey. In later life, once he was a rising general, it became the object of his faithful staff to prevent this from happening and to conceal it when they failed to prevent it. Drinking did not make Grant cheerful—indeed his hangovers were made more acute both by his tendency toward migraine headaches, which was exacerbated by alcohol, and by shame at his own weakness in taking to the bottle.

To some degree, fame and a sense of purpose overcame Grant's drinking problem after 1861, and the presence of Mrs. Grant usually appears to have kept him from the bottle. He was not a man who could withstand his own failure or Julia's absence: It was as simple as that. At Fort Vancouver, however, he could not escape his own failure; he had no sense of purpose; and Julia was fifteen hundred impassable miles away, so he drank. Whether he drank as much as, or less than, people said hardly matters.

Transferred eventually to Fort Humboldt in Northern California, he was lonelier still—he did not even have a horse of his own to ride—and his drinking soon came to the attention of his commanding officer. Ordered to give it up, he tried hard; then he went back to drinking, and finally, in the spring of 1854, he took the drastic step of writing a letter resigning from the army, either under pressure from his commander or out of despair, ironically receiving by letter his promotion to captain on the same day. The captaincy had come too late to make a difference to Grant. His only thought was to get home, explain himself to Julia, and never leave her side again. With at last a purpose in mind, Grant set off as fast as he could, borrowing money for the journey from his West Point classmate Simon Bolivar Buckner. Grant was a civilian again for the first time since the day he had arrived at West Point.

Whatever Julia's thoughts about the matter, Jesse was determined to set matters right. He, better than anyone, knew how unfit Ulysses was for anything other than soldiering, and was appalled at his son's throwing away his career, however modest it might be. Jesse wrote at once to his congressman (not the unlucky Hamer this time) to request that the secretary of war reinstate his son Ulysses as a captain, and when that failed to have any effect, followed it up with a letter of his own. The secretary of war wrote back a rather snubbing letter pointing out that it was too late, that his decision on the matter was irrevocable, and suggesting between the lines that there were matters Captain Grant would probably prefer not to face publicly—perhaps a reference to rumors of his drinking on duty, perhaps to the missing thousand dollars.

The secretary of war at the time was, of all people, Jefferson Davis, future president of the Confederacy, and the one man, apart from General Hancock, whom Ulysses Grant in later life would treat as a personal enemy. Hancock, Grant forgave as he lay dying; Davis, who had snubbed Grant's father, refused to reinstate Grant in the army, and then gone on and betrayed his own country to lead the Confederacy, Grant could never forgive.

After a good deal of correspondence and unnecessary travel back and forth between New York City and Sackets Harbor, Grant finally rejoined Julia in St. Louis, a failure at the early age of thirty-two, with no trade beyond the one he had just resigned. Since no help was forthcoming from Jesse, who did not disguise his feeling that Ulysses had thrown away a perfectly good position, or feel like supporting not only Ulysses but Julia and their two children (with a third already on the way), Grant was obliged to throw himself on the mercy of his father-in-law, and took over some of his brother-in-law's farmland in Kentucky. With his own hands Grant built a house, which he called, with some accuracy (and perhaps a degree of irony), "Hardscrabble," tilled the soil, and put in a crop. Julia adapted to this life of primitive yeoman farming—the kind of thing Jefferson had dreamed of as the backbone of the infant republic, but from which everybody who tried it was eager to escape—but she did not pretend to like it. She called the house "crude," as indeed it was, and does not seem to have had much confidence in Ulysses' ability to survive as a farmer, even with the help of the Dent family slaves. She would soon be proved correct.

Grant's log cabin

The presence of the slaves may have taught Grant something about the notorious inefficiency of slave labor—after all, hard work gained the slave nothing—but it did not save the farm. Still, the Grants survived nearly two years of backbreaking labor, poor returns, and mounting debt, while she bore him two more children, a girl, Nellie, and another boy, Jesse, named after Ulysses' father—a sentimental gesture that failed to soften the old man's heart.

Once again it was not for lack of hard work that Grant failed as a farmer—it was the *business* of farming that defeated him. He could do anything that was needed on the farm, it appeared, except make a profit out of it.

To some degree that was not his fault. "Manifest Destiny" had increased the power of Wall Street, and the world of high finance and railway building, over that of Jeffersonian yeomen, small farmers, and pioneers. The time had come "to pay the piper" for the enormous increase in America's size, many times larger than what had been acquired by the Louisiana Purchase, and requiring huge amounts of capital for what we would now call "development," in a nation with a largely unregulated banking system. As a result bank crises and a sharp decline in agricultural prices ruined many small farmers shrewder than Grant.

While he had been planting his crops and building Hardscrabble, the consequences of the annexation of Texas and victory over Mexico had been coming home to roost. The United States was now a continental nation, but the question of slavery still divided it. Mrs. Grant might gush over the loyalty and affection to her person of the Dent family slaves, but the burning question of whether slavery could be extended to the new territories of the West still perplexed and infuriated Americans. Slavery was no longer a debating issue but a *fighting* one.

In the North abolitionists took the gloves off. Mrs. Harriet Beecher Stowe wrote *Uncle Tom's Cabin*, the book that caused Queen Victoria to cry, that made Simon Legree the symbol of Southern oppression, and that would eventually cause Lincoln to say to its author, on meeting her, "So you're the little woman who wrote the book that made this great war!" The North reacted with outrage to the U.S. Supreme Court's decision, in the Dred Scott case, that a slave was merely property who could be hunted down and returned to his owner, even from the North. On the floor of the U.S. Senate, distinguished senators slashed at each other with canes, and members of both houses took to carrying Col. Samuel Colt's new pocket revolver. And in the Kansas Territory, "Bleeding Kansas," the question of whether slavery could be—*would* be—extended farther West was beginning to be played out in blood, not just ink.

It is against this background of rising tension and anger that Ulysses Grant's failure as a farmer must be seen. Like the rest of the nation, he was waiting, appalled and impotent, for the storm to break. He could not have predicted the swift and dreadful chain of events—the spiraling outbreak of murder and lawlessness between abolitionist and proslavery factions in Kansas, culminating in the fearful outrage enacted by the followers of John Brown and his sons on the hapless slave-owning farmers at Pottawatomie Creek, whom Brown dragged from their beds and executed with a broadsword—the fearful plunge toward civil war that had been set in motion by the victories that Grant had helped to win. Still it was there, like a thunderstorm building over the plains, distant but threatening, and only the deaf failed to hear the ominous rumbling.[1]

These events did not, of course, take place at once, but sputtered, like a burning fuse, over nearly a decade of increasing acrimony and sporadic, often gleeful, butchery on the part of fanatics on both sides, as a war of words hardened into the prospect of a real war—perhaps the only profession for which Captain Grant, failed farmer and small entrepreneur, was properly trained. All over the country the state militias drilled, mostly clumsy country bumpkins, clueless; without uniforms; sometimes shoeless; armed, if at all, with weapons that went back to the War of 1812;

guided, if they were lucky, by some old textbook on infantry drill in the hands of one of their elected officers; and by a firm belief in the national myth of the Minute Men at Concord and Lexington, the amateur soldiers who had left their homes and farms, hunting rifles in hand, to confront the Redcoats.

In the meantime Grant, having failed at farming, was forced to undergo the ultimate humiliation. In the summer of 1860 he was obliged to turn back to his father, tail between his legs, and ask for help. Jesse's terms were harsh and not negotiable. The Grants could come back and live in Galena, Illinois, and Ulysses would work as a clerk in Jesse's harness and leather shop there, under the supervision of his younger brothers, Orvil and Simpson.

Like many other writers, F. Scott Fitzgerald, in *The Great Gatsby*, speculated on Grant "lolling in his general store in Galena" as the prototype of the seemingly ordinary American waiting patiently to be called to a high destiny, but it cannot have appeared so to Grant, or anybody else in Galena. His salary was small and grudgingly paid; he and his family lived in a tiny house, which Julia could have compared with White Haven only with great dissatisfaction—an Irish maid was no substitute for a bevy of slave house servants—and Grant's total lack of any of those qualities that make for a good salesman were only too obvious, to both his brothers and the customers. Even those in Galena who did not think he was a secret drinker—and they were few—could hardly fail to notice his dull, vacant expression, his shuffling gait, his threadbare clothes, and his total lack of interest in the leather and harness business.

Burdened with debts, stuck at last in his father's leather business, which he had always sought to avoid, with no prospects and not even a horse to ride, he waited—for what? In the leather shop the customers talked about the news and politics, and Grant listened silently, tying packages with twine and perhaps making the occasional sale. He had no gift for small talk, and he kept his opinions to himself, but we know from his memoirs what those opinions were. He had opposed the Mexican War, he was against the expansion of slavery, he thought President James Buchanan was a weakling, and he was moving from being a Democrat to becoming a Lincoln Republican. Above all, he recognized what few other people had thought through yet: If the Southern states seceded from the Union, there would be war; if there was war one result would eventually be the destruction of slavery; and that war, if and when it came, would be incalculably more bloody than anyone supposed, and would be won only by brute force and killing on a scale that would eclipse all previous wars.

The election of Abraham Lincoln set in motion the events that were to bring Ulysses S. Grant out from behind the counter of the harness shop for good. On April 15 the news of the firing on Fort Sumter reached Galena, and a mass meeting was called by local congressman Elihu B. Washburne, a Galena man, at which Grant was present. Two days later another meeting was held, to discuss the recruitment of troops. As the only man in town who was a graduate of West Point, Grant was asked to chair the meeting and did so. In his own words, "I never went into our leather store after that meeting, to put up a package or do other business."

Grant's star had not yet risen, but it was about to, and would carry him away from Galena and into such fame as few men have experienced. For once he moved with a sure step. He went, still in his shabby civilian clothes, and at his own expense, with the company of Galena volunteers to Springfield, where they were to be mustered, and declined to advance himself for the captaincy on the grounds that as a former officer of the Regular Army he was entitled to something better—a stroke of cunning and realism that was new to Grant but may simply have been the instinctive understanding of how the army works coming back to him, a West

Pointer and regular officer, as if he had never taken off the uniform. For weeks Grant was in limbo, a civilian in a volunteer army that was slowly being put into uniform, with no rank or position. Looking at his Galena volunteers, he might have agreed with the Duke of Wellington's comment on the first sight of his troops in the Peninsula: "I do not know what effect they will have on the enemy, sir, but by God, they frighten *me*!" He lobbied his old senior officers of the Mexican War days, with no result; he paid two calls on Maj. Gen. George B. McClellan, whom he had known at West Point, and was twice ignored, left waiting and rebuffed; he begged Jesse to intercede for him and seek an appointment for him as a colonel; then finally, almost by accident, Grant himself hit upon the right lever to pull, and went back to Galena to seek the support of Representative Washburne, who saw in Grant something nobody else had seen (except Julia): a rare degree of determination, real experience of war, and, perhaps most important to Washburne, the fact that here was a fellow Galena man, somebody who would be grateful to the politician who gave him a push.

Grant returned to Springfield, and on June 17, in his own matter-of-fact way, was able to write home that he had been appointed a colonel.

The war was about to begin in earnest.

CHAPTER

5

rant may have been a colonel, but he still had no uniform or horse. Opportunity had knocked before he was kitted out for it. The officers of the Twenty-first Illinois Volunteers, which had been formed at Mattoon, had complained bitterly to the governor that their commanding officer was incompetent and drunk, and when it was clear that they meant business (and were probably correct), the governor suggested Colonel Grant to replace him. Grant arrived to take command of his regiment in wrinkled civilian clothes and a battered hat, and found them "ragged and barefoot themselves," as well as undisciplined. The uncertainty and sense of failure that had haunted him as a civilian seemed to drop away from him instantly. Men who were insolent to officers he had tied to posts and, when necessary, gagged; foul language he punished severely; saluting he insisted upon. Very shortly the Twenty-first became a model regiment, except for Grant himself, who still had no uniform, military equipment, or horse. His father, Jesse, and his brothers were not prepared to put up another penny toward Ulysses' military career, while his father-in-law now considered him a traitor to the Southern cause and made it clear that while there would always be a place at his table for Julia, there would henceforth be none for Ulysses (ironically, Colonel Dent would end up living in the White House as a kind of perma-nent house guest once Grant became president, surprising people with his staunchly Confederate views). Eventually a Galena merchant took pity on Grant and loaned him enough money for his uniform and equipment, and Grant took the Twenty-first to war.

Grant marched his regiment into Missouri in search of rebels, particularly a certain Col. Thomas Harris, whose Confederate troops were plaguing local farmers and who was said to be a fiery and aggressive commander. Grant located Harris's camp and advanced on it, writing years later that, as he led his men over the brow of a hill, "I would have given anything to be back in Illinois, but I had not the moral courage to halt."

He soon discovered that Harris and his men had already fled, and wrote, "It occurred to me at once that Harris was much afraid of me as I had been of him. This was a view of the question that I had never taken before; but it was one I never forgot afterwards."

Henceforth Grant would always operate on the assumption that the enemy had as much reason to be afraid of him as he might be of the enemy, and "from that event to the end of the war, I never experienced trepidation upon confronting an enemy."

Grant's memoirs are pellucid and reveal not only a striking literary gift but an amazing memory; still, his modesty is such that he has to be read carefully. He is not writing here about fear or physical courage—he had already demonstrated his fearlessness in Mexico to his own satisfaction—he is writing here about what amounts to "stage fright" as a commander of men in battle. He had learned a lot by observing Zachary Taylor in Mexico, but as every young officer discovers in battle, it is one thing to give an order and quite another to know it will be obeyed. Here, in the unpromising countryside of Missouri, he had braced himself to order his men into battle, led them over "the brow of the hill," and found, to his relief and theirs, that the enemy had fled. It was his first step as a commander—the realization that he knew what he was doing and that his men would follow him—that Grant was describing here, exactly like that of Napoleon at the bridge of Arcola, when the young Napoleon, who was as personally fearless as Grant, also realized for the first time that men would follow him.

It may be too that Grant at last realized his own strengths. He was not a thinker, like the unfortunate General McClellan, who thought so long and hard about a campaign that it never got anywhere, leading Lincoln to complain that McClellan had "a case of the slows," and exasperating the president until he finally asked if he could borrow the Army of the Potomac since McClellan wasn't using it. Grant, on the contrary, was a man of action, and movement was what stimulated him, not thought. He would try something, and if it failed he would try something else, but his instinct was always to keep moving forward against the enemy.

Napoleon, when asked what his method was of beginning a battle, replied, *"On s'engage, et puis on voit."* Much as Grant, according to his memoirs, disliked Napoleon, his view of battle was the same—he attacked the enemy, and then he waited to see what happened. One senses in the words of Grant's about his anticlimactic attack on Harris, a dawning understanding that he had found, at last, something he could do better than other men. He was courageous, he had common sense, he could read a map, and, like the child he had been, he would never go backward and retrace his steps once he had started out. In an army full of commanders busily planning how to win a war without fighting a battle, Grant sought one out. The elements of military genius were all there, hardened and annealed by the experience of Mexico and the years of failure—now at last he had the opportunity to use them.

While Grant marched his men up and down the dusty Missouri roads in pursuit of Harris, larger events were taking place in Springfield and Washington, D.C. President Lincoln was anxious to create enough brigadier generals to command the rapidly growing volunteer army, and Representative Washburne, a fellow Illinois politician, convinced the president that at least one of these new generals should come from his own district. Lincoln, who never forgot the rule that "all politics are local," allowed Washburne to name his pick. Since Grant was the only Galena man appointed a colonel, Washburne put his name down for promotion to the rank of brigadier general, and by the time Grant returned from the fruitless chase after Harris he read in the newspaper that he was now Brig. Gen. Ulysses S. Grant.

Only a few months ago he had been ex-captain Sam Grant, slouching behind the counter of his father's store, wrapping packages. Now, he wore the single star of a brigadier general on his shoulders and, surrounded by his staff, rode into Cairo, Illinois, to set up his headquarters at the Cairo Hotel, which no less an authority than W. H. Russell, the famous war correspondent of the London *Times*, would describe as a hellhole of heat, vermin, and flies.

Russell's interest in Cairo, Illinois, like Grant's, is a point worth noting. At this early stage of the Civil War, the belief on both sides was that one big battle would bring the other side to its senses. If nothing else the first Battle of Bull Run (or First Manassas, as it is known in the South) would shortly prove that this assumption was doubtful. Fought within sight of Washington, D.C., in what are now its suburbs, Bull Run was a devastating defeat for the North. Crowds of civilians came out by carriage to see the battle, as if it were a parade, and saw Brig. Gen. Irvin McDowell's army be badly mauled by the army of Brig. Gen. P. G. T. Beauregard. McDowell lost nearly three thousand men and twenty-seven cannon, as most of his troops broke and ran. A determined pursuit might have won Beauregard Washington, but the victorious Confederates were as exhausted as their defeated opponents.

Three things emerged from the disaster that would affect the future course of the war. One was the first appearance on the battlefield of Confederate brigadier general Thomas J. Jackson, one of the great generals of the war, who earned his nickname, "Stonewall," at Bull Run, when Gen. Barnard E. Bee rallied his troops by shouting, "There is Jackson standing like a stone wall." The second was the belief, in the North and in the South, that the war would be won—*must* be won—in the narrow territory that separated Washington from Richmond. And the third was the very slowly dawning realization that neither side would give way after one big battle, and that many more might have to be fought.

Grant (and W. H. Russell, who had seen war at its best and its worst in the Crimea, where he had personally witnessed the Charge of the Light Brigade from a position next to Lord Raglan himself) understood almost at once that the key to winning the war was in the West, not in the East, in front of Washington.[1] He saw that the Confederacy's weakness was its size, not its industrial inferiority to the North. The Confederacy was vast, and there was no way it could be defended with equal strength all along its frontier, yet this was exactly what Jefferson Davis proposed to do. Davis wanted a big victory—big enough to shock Lincoln to the bargaining table for a treaty of peace, and to convince the European powers that the Confederacy was there to stay—but he also didn't want to surrender an inch of territory for fear of what that might do to Southern morale. Though something of a bookworm at West Point and afterward, Davis seemed to have forgotten that old military maxim "To attempt to be strong everywhere is to be strong nowhere."

Seen from drab, dusty Cairo, the heart of the South lay open to a determined thrust, aimed down the great rivers that separated the Confederacy into two separate regions. A determined advance through the border states of Missouri and Kentucky would bring a Federal army within reach of Tennessee and Mississippi, and such a thrust could be supplied by river rather than overland. Victory would split the Confederacy, expose its vast, weakly defended western border to attack at any point, and allow a Union army to threaten the Southern heartland, opening up a war of movement instead of big, set-piece battles. Grant might not have spent much time on books about strategy at West Point, but he could read a map, which is more than could be said for many of his colleagues. From Cairo he could see how to win the war, as plain as a pikestaff.

Russell saw it, too, hence his interest in Cairo. And, more important, a thousand miles to the east, Abraham Lincoln saw it—felt it in his bones—for, after all, he was an Illinois man, who had traveled up and down the great rivers in his youth. He sensed, uneasily, that McDowell had been wrong, that even General Scott was wrong, and that McClellan would be wrong, too, when his turn came, and looked to the West for a general who understood what was in the back of his mind: a whole different kind of war.

For the moment no such person seemed to exist. Grant's immediate superior was the flamboyant Maj. Gen. John C. Frémont, "the Pathfinder," as he was called, after his supposed explorations in the West, a political and celebrity general, an amateur, whose personal fortune, glamorous wife, and undisguised presidential ambitions did not inspire much confidence in Lincoln. Frémont was too busy talking to reporters to pay much attention to Grant, whom he scarcely knew, and thus was unable to prevent Grant from taking his forces forty miles above Cairo to seize the town of Paducah, Kentucky, before the Confederates got there. Paducah was not of itself much of a prize, but a look at the map shows that the Tennessee and the Cumberland Rivers both flow into the Ohio near Paducah. A Union army could descend* the two rivers deep into the heart of Tennessee.

The Confederates could read a map, too, and they had already built two strong forts, Fort Henry to protect the Tennessee River, and Fort Donelson to protect the Cumberland, and manned them with sizable forces. It now occurred to them that occupying Paducah would strengthen their position, but the force they sent to take it retired when they found Grant

*In fact, due to the peculiarities of geography, both of these rivers run northward. I use the word "descend" because Grant would be going southward, but he would be moving against the current.

already holding it. Not a shot had been fired, but Grant had opened the way South just a crack, and calmed the good citizens of Paducah with a respectful and sensible proclamation, appealing to their better instincts. "I have come among you," he wrote, "not as an enemy, but as your friend and fellow-citizen," and when Lincoln saw it, he is reported to have said, "The man who can write like that is fitted to command in the West."

Grant's soothing proclamation was followed by a more rousing one from Frémont, threatening among other things to seize the slaves and property of Confederate sympathizers and shoot any man not in uniform found bearing a gun. These were exactly the kind of sentiments most calculated to turn inhabitants of the "border states" away from the Union cause at just the moment when Lincoln was trying to woo them, and when Frémont high-handedly refused to withdraw his proclamation at the president's request, he was removed from his command, his presidential aspirations as good as gone.

Grant was no longer in Frémont's shadow, and his name was beginning to be known, at least in the White House. Lincoln may not have said, when told about Grant's drinking, "Tell me the brand of whiskey that Grant drinks—I would like to send a barrel of it to every one of my other generals," but he *did* say to one of Grant's many critics, "I cannot spare this man—he fights."

Grant would shortly prove that he could not only fight but move fast. In the meantime, with the collapse of Frémont's balloon, Grant found himself under the command of Maj. Gen. Henry W. Halleck, commander of the Department of Missouri. Up until then Halleck's chief concern had not been the Confederates but the more important task of getting rid of Frémont and maintaining his superiority in numbers over his rival, Brig. Gen. Don Carlos Buell, commander of the Department of Ohio, but Grant now moved into Halleck's field of vision as a new threat. Halleck was known to his fellow army officers as "Old Brains," and he didn't like or trust a single thing he had heard about Grant. Cautious, pop-eyed, bald, quick to criticize, and slow to make up his mind, a deskbound general who was something of an intriguer and a gossip (many of the stories about Grant's drinking can be traced back to him), Halleck was to become, for a time, Grant's *bête noire*, though once Grant finally succeeded he would find Halleck a useful man to look after things in Washington while Grant took to the field. Halleck's strengths—attention to detail, administrative ability, a love of paperwork, and an intimate knowledge of the army way of doing things—in many ways complemented Grant's.

The second person who entered Grant's life at this point, and made an immediate difference, was John A. Rawlins, who joined Grant's staff as an aide. Grant did not know Rawlins well—for some time he wrote his name as "Rollins"—but Rawlins was a fellow Galena man and had in fact been the attorney for Jesse Grant's leather and harness shop.

Rawlins took charge of Grant's chaotic paperwork, for which Grant had no gift at all. He also acted, from the beginning, as Grant's *éminence bleue*—adviser, protector, sounding board. Rawlins was abrasive, exacting, even abusive, had no difficulty (unlike Grant) in saying no to people, and was above all a fervent and outspoken "teetotaler," who abstained from all forms of spirits. Rawlins was a born follower, who had been looking all his life for a man to follow and found him in Grant. It became his role to prevent Grant from reaching for the bottle, and on those occasions when he failed, to keep Grant out of sight. Rawlins was like a faithful guard dog, ferocious, absolutely loyal to his master, and devoted to protecting him, even from himself.

With Rawlins to guard his flank, Grant took to the field immediately. Ordered by Halleck to make "a demonstration" at Belmont, a Confederate camp on the Mississippi, twenty miles below Cairo, opposite Columbus, Missouri—that is, to impress and overawe the Confederates there by his presence—Grant went beyond his orders. He took three thousand men downriver by steamer and decided to attack Belmont instead. He landed, drove the Confederates out of the fortified camp, then was sharply driven back himself when they counterattacked in superior numbers. Grant had stirred up a hornet's nest and was very lucky to get his troops embarked again.

Grant was the last man to leave, riding his horse straight down a steep, almost "perpendicular" bank under enemy fire, then across a narrow plank onto the deck of the waiting steamer—another brilliant feat of horsemanship that would have been performed by a stuntman in a movie. No sooner was Grant in his cabin than a bullet came through the hull, hitting the pillow on which he was about to lay his head. He must have begun to sense in himself a certain destiny, but also, as he began to suspect at Belmont, and perhaps even in Mexico, a gift for command. Risks did not seem to scare him. He hardly even noticed danger. Quietly but firmly he got things done.

Halleck bristled at Grant's transformation of a demonstration into an amphibious landing against a larger force, but Grant, with a newly acquired sense of public relations, or perhaps on Rawlins's shrewd advice, decided to call it "a raid." If it had been an *attack*, then he had been repulsed, as the Confederates claimed, whereas if it was a *raid*, it had been daring and successful. Halleck grumbled, was not fooled for a moment, but accepted Grant's explanation, though it did nothing to increase his confidence in Grant.

Nevertheless, after considerable acrimonious correspondence between Halleck and Grant, and a few suggestions leaked from Halleck to Washington that Grant might have been drunk, Halleck reluctantly agreed to let his impetuous subordinate attack Fort Henry, the weaker of the two Confederate forts that guarded the Tennessee and the Cumberland Rivers, surely hoping to upstage General Buell and, perhaps wrongly, assuming that this would keep Grant occupied for some time.

SECESSION ORDNANCE STORES

PLAN OF F T HENRY

TENNESSEE RIV.

BURSTED RIFLED 24 POUNDER.

THE ATTACK ON FORT HENRY.

Buell had 45,000 men in his command, just south of Louisville, Kentucky, and had been promising to advance on Nashville for some time. Halleck, with 91,000 men, and an eye fixed firmly on Washington, wanted very much to carry out an attack before Buell did. Buell's forces were spread out, and he was in no hurry to move them, and Halleck must have thought there could be no harm in dispatching Grant to do a little mischief in the general direction of Nashville before Buell did.

Grant did not hesitate. He moved, like Rommel nearly eighty years later, *mit blitzartiger Schnelle*, the lightning speed so favored by German Panzer generals, and took the Confederates by surprise. Grant was carried south on the Tennessee River by a flotilla of transports and gunboats, under the command of Comm. Andrew H. Foote, U.S.N., which had originally been assembled to carry Buell south, and was still waiting for Buell to move.

Having preempted Buell's flotilla, Grant now deftly stepped into the limelight before Buell. He was about to receive help from an unexpected source—his Confederate opponents. Despite his dislike of Napoleon, Grant was about to prove the emperor right again. When asked what kind of generals he liked best, Napoleon is said to have replied, "Lucky ones." Luck was about to strike Grant at last.

Though the Confederacy had recognized the importance of the rivers flowing north into the Ohio before the Union generals did, its choice of positions for the forts defending them was hampered by a reluctance to advance too far north into Kentucky, and the Confederate fortress system was therefore built at unpromising points. Perhaps Jefferson Davis and Gen. A. S. Johnston had also dozed during the lectures on fortifications at West Point, or neglected to read Vauban's classic work on the subject, but in any case Fort Henry, on the Tennessee River, was placed on low ground, so that it could be shelled by gunboats. The Confederates then made the classic mistake of attempting to strengthen it by building a supporting fort—Fort Heiman—on the opposite, west bank of the Tennessee, which was on higher ground but only lightly manned.

Had they paid more attention at West Point to reading Vauban, Louis XIV's builder of fortifications, they would have realized the folly of trying to reinforce a poor position with a weak one, but Grant saw the opportunity at once. He landed Brig. Gen. Charles F. Smith—a crusty, competent, "scientific" soldier, who by coincidence had been Grant's chief instructor at West Point—on the west bank of the Tennessee about two miles north of Fort Heiman, and the Confederate commander immediately abandoned it. That left Fort Henry exposed to fire from Foote's gunboats and to an overland enveloping attack carried out swiftly by Grant, so Fort Henry too was abandoned, its 2,500-man garrison marching on two dirt tracks over muddy, rugged country to join the Confederate forces at Fort Donelson, on the west bank of the Cumberland.

Grant took the opportunity of sending Smith, who seemed to relish having escaped from his teaching position at West Point into real warfare, to destroy the Memphis & Ohio railroad bridge over the Tennessee, in effect stranding the Confederates; then moved his forces through cold, wet weather and thick mud in two columns to invest Fort Donelson.

He had taken Fort Heiman on February 4, he took Fort Henry on the sixth, and he had surrounded nearly twenty thousand Confederate troops in Fort Donelson by the fourteenth. By the night of February 15–16, Grant's left wing, under Smith, pierced the elaborate Confederate defenses, and Confederate generals John Floyd and Gideon Pillow fled, abandoning command to the hapless Buckner, who surrendered to Grant on the sixteenth, after their famous exchange of correspondence.[2]

Thus in twelve days Grant had opened up the way into Tennessee, captured the largest number of Confederate prisoners and guns since the war began—it was in fact the largest surrender in the history of North America to date—and achieved the first major Union victory of the war.

Grant's troops were now only seventy miles from Nashville, and within a few days, as the news traveled north by telegraph, he would be proclaimed a national hero by the press and promoted to major general of volunteers.

Because he smoked cigars (when he could afford them), admiring citizens sent him cigars by the box—a tidal wave of tobacco that would continue to the end of his life. He became, like Freud and Winston Churchill in a later age, a chain smoker of cigars, seldom photographed without one; in the end, like Freud, he would die of his addiction, from cancer of the jaw and throat.

But in 1862 that was far in the future. Grant did not have long to enjoy his success. No sooner had he put up his second star than he was in trouble again. Buell, taking advantage of Grant's victories, at last moved to take Nashville, and was followed there by Grant, who had been named "Commander of the Military Department of Western Tennessee"—a title that was vague but implied that he was Buell's superior officer. This provoked Halleck, who must have felt that he had created a monster, to complain to the new general in chief in Washington, George B. McClellan, who had replaced the ailing Scott (and in whose waiting room Grant had twice sat fruitlessly waiting for an interview), that Grant had quit his command to go to Nashville, failed to keep him (Halleck) informed, and was probably drinking again. McClellan wired back that Halleck should "not hesitate to arrest him at once," but Halleck contented himself with giving Gen. C. F. Smith command of the advance into Tennessee, while ordering a shaken Grant to remain at Fort Henry to await further investigation.

Grant finally managed to smooth Halleck's ruffled feathers; the rumors of his drinking were disposed of by Rawlins—although there remains a strong possibility that they were true—and by March 1862 Grant was once again headed south, in command of forty thousand troops. Smith seems to have taken all this intrigue calmly and was happy enough to give up a command he had never sought—Grant had not been one of his more successful pupils at West Point, but he seems to have recognized in him superior qualities of leadership. Grant's commanders now included at least two unusual characters, Brig. Gen. William Tecumseh Sherman, temporarily in disgrace and assumed by many to be insane, but who would soon rise to become one of the most successful Union generals, and Lew Wallace, the future author of *Ben Hur* and governor of the Territory of New Mexico, who would play a leading role in ending the career of Billy the Kid.

Halleck had finally managed to achieve overall command of the area and conceived a plan in which Buell and Grant (once he was restored to command) would move south, meet at Pittsburg Landing on the Tennessee, and concentrate their forces, then push on to Memphis. This plan was jeopardized almost at once by Buell's slowness—it is possible that Buell had not forgiven Grant for preempting his flotilla and his limelight to undertake the attack on Fort Henry—so that Grant arrived at Pittsburg Landing before Buell, to face a larger Confederate force under the command of Generals A. S. Johnston and P. G. T. Beauregard.

Whether Grant was drinking or not remains open to question, but he was certainly not at his best. It may be that the quarrel with Halleck and the temporary loss of his command had shaken his confidence, or that Julia Grant was still on her way south to be with him, or that he wasn't confident that Buell would arrive in time to be of any use. Or it may simply be that Rawlins's concentration was focused elsewhere and that Grant had access to whiskey again (the one item that was never in short supply in both armies). For whatever reason, Grant spread his forces out loosely on the south side of the Tennessee River, and placed his own headquarters at Savannah, nine miles west (and downstream) of Pittsburg Landing, and on the opposite side of the river, which meant that he had to commute back and forth by river steamer every day. He later claimed that he was waiting anxiously for the arrival of Buell, who had agreed to meet him at Savannah, but that seems unlikely—word could have been left there for Buell to ride down to Pittsburg Landing as soon as he arrived, and it is just faintly possible that Grant didn't want to risk anybody in his army seeing him drunk. In any event he seems to have had no idea that the Confederate forces were concentrating at Corinth and moving directly toward Pittsburg Landing to drive his army into the river.

The first warning the army received came in the late afternoon of Saturday, April 5, in the shape of thousands of terrified rabbits and deer, clearly being driven through the woods by something, which began to run through the Union encampments. Behind the fleeing wildlife were more than 41,000 Confederate soldiers, who had marched out of Corinth and were now within two miles of the Union lines. Several sharp firefights took place that night between outlying Union troops and Confederate skirmishers, but nobody seems to have bothered to inform Grant, who was nine miles away and had unwisely telegraphed Halleck before going to bed: "I have scarcely the faintest idea of an attack being made upon us." Only a few miles away Johnston dismissed Beauregard's more cautious appraisal of the Confederate situation by saying, "I would fight them if they were a million!"

Good as his word, at dawn Johnston attacked, flinging his full forces against the Federals—most of whom were only just waking up or boiling their coffee—in one long, extended savage blow that took Grant's whole army by surprise, as well as Grant himself, who heard the firing as he breakfasted. Still ignorant of where Buell was with his twenty thousand men, Grant limped on board a steamer—he had taken a severe fall from his horse a few days earlier—and set off toward Pittsburg Landing. He stopped at Crump's Landing, where he had inadvisably placed Lew Wallace, to order Wallace to advance toward Pittsburg Landing—Wallace, as ill informed as Grant, took the wrong road, however, and thus left Grant short of five thousand men—then proceeded toward the ever-increasing noise of heavy fire, concern and some confusion evident on his face to those who accompanied him.

The closer Grant got, the more obvious it was to him how badly he had miscalculated. It was late in the morning when he finally arrived at Pittsburg Landing, and from the river, and even from the shore once he had landed, he could see nothing. In the age before smokeless gunpowder, the battlefield was obscured by clouds of dense, gritty smoke, and in any case Grant was looking up at a seemingly impenetrable thicket of scrub and second growth, from which thousands of panicked Union troops were emerging, with or without their weapons, to huddle beside the river.

Now that Grant realized he had allowed himself to be outwitted by Johnston, he was calm again. He would have agreed with Wellington's appraisal of his situation before Waterloo, "By God, Bonaparte has humbugged me!" and, also like Wellington, who had to hold out all day until Blücher arrived with his Prussians, Grant would have to hang on by the skin of his teeth until Buell arrived to join *him*. Since his cavalry was useless in the rough, heavily wooded country, bisected by creeks and streams, Grant ordered them to round up the Union stragglers and drive them back to plug the gaps in the battle lines. Having done this, he sent messengers off to look for Buell, and went forward to have a closer look. Nothing he saw was encouraging—he would later remark that in places the dead lay so thick and close to each other it would have been possible to walk across a field without putting a foot on the ground—and from all accounts his left was being pushed back to the river, without any sign that the Confederate advance was slowing.

By noon, however, Sherman—ever the optimist—had reported more hopeful signs, and by one o'clock Buell himself finally appeared and met with Grant aboard his steamer. Grant urged Buell into action, and for once Buell moved quickly, and by late afternoon, the Confederate rush had been slowed by a series of fierce artillery clashes and vicious hand-to-hand fighting. Grant did not know it yet, but luck had touched him again. Confederate general A. S. Johnston had been hit in the thigh; thinking it was a minor wound, he ignored it, continuing to urge his troops forward. When his staff finally got him off his horse and pulled his boot off, it was full of blood. It was too late to save Johnston, who bled to death on the battlefield, and command passed to Beauregard, who had not shared Johnston's optimism about the attack in the first place.

With Johnston's death the steam went out of the Confederate attack. As the dreadful day ended in a torrential rainstorm, Grant took refuge in a battlefield hospital, but he could not stand the blood, the screams, and the cries of the wounded and the dying (shades of the tannery), and took shelter under a tree. Sherman found him there in the dark, whittling a stick with his pocketknife and smoking a cigar, his hat pulled low over his eyes. As the story goes, Sherman said, "Well, Grant, we've had the devil's own day, haven't we?" Grant went on whittling and, without looking up, said, "Yes, lick 'em tomorrow, though."

And so it would prove. Grant attacked in the morning—now, he finally had all Buell's twenty thousand men and Wallace's five thousand, the author of *Ben Hur* having at last found his way to the battlefield—drove the Confederates back, and by nightfall they were back in Corinth again. Shiloh was, to that date, the biggest battle ever fought on American soil, and the casualties came to nearly thirty thousand killed, wounded, and missing. More Americans were killed at Shiloh than in all previous American wars combined—the Revolutionary War, the War of 1812, and the Mexican War—a grim statistic that was to shock both the North and the South alike.

Grant, though Shiloh was not his finest moment as a general, had at least not been paralyzed by Johnston's surprise attack or by the sheer ferocity of the fighting, as Burnside would be at Fredericksburg, and Hooker at Chancellorsville. He had dispersed his forces poorly, reacted slowly, and arrived on the scene late, but once he was there he didn't lose his nerve. He stood his ground against superior numbers and won.

Nevertheless his victory brought down upon his head a torrent of criticism and abuse. The "butcher's bill" of Shiloh, once it reached the press, fueled speculation that Grant had been caught napping, that he had deployed his forces ineptly, that he had been incapacitated by drink. Newspapers and members of Congress called for an investigation, while Halleck, shaken by the storm of criticism, did not attempt to defend Grant—quite the contrary.

Grant did little to defend himself—perhaps on the wise advice of Rawlins—and stayed as silent as Achilles in his tent, though he toyed with the idea of resigning from the army until talked out of it by Sherman. In time the storm blew over, chiefly because Lincoln never lost his confidence in Grant, and also because it began to dawn on people that Shiloh, however bloody, was a victory, and that the war would not be won without casualties.

When Jesse Grant, enraged at the criticism of his son, took to writing furious letters to the newspapers defending him, Grant wrote his father a firm letter that made it clear that the son was now grown up. "I have not an enemy in the world who has done me so much injury as you in your efforts at my defense. I require no defenders and for my sake let me alone. . . . Do nothing to correct what you have already done, but for the future keep quiet upon this subject."[3] It is hard not to sense the satisfaction with which Grant must have written this letter.

Demoted to Halleck's second in command, Grant glumly accompanied Halleck on a tortuously slow advance toward Corinth, Mississippi—Halleck, once out from behind his desk, moved at a snail's pace—until news came that Halleck had been ordered to Washington to replace McClellan as general in chief, a job that might, in fact, have been made to order for him, and at which he would excel—while Grant was to replace him as commander of Union forces in the West.

He was now, at last, in charge.

CHAPTER

6

No sooner did Grant have what he wanted—or appeared to want—than he slipped into one of his periodic slumps. In the fall of 1862 Halleck was in faraway Washington, Grant was deep in Mississippi, the outrage over the casualties at Shiloh was beginning to die down, put into perspective by what appeared to be an endless series of costly and shameful Union defeats at the hands of Robert E. Lee in the East, Mrs. Grant had joined him, and there was even talk, which would soon be fulfilled, of making Grant a major general in the Regular Army, as opposed to a mere major general of volunteers. On the other hand Grant now found himself military commander in an area almost the size of western Europe, with social, political, and military problems that would have daunted Caesar. To say that Grant was not equipped for this role is putting it mildly. His previous experience in administration, after all, had been as a quartermaster of army supplies in the small garrison of Fort Vancouver and as a clerk wrapping packages in his father's shop in Galena, under the watchful eyes of his younger brothers. His generals seemed unsure whether Grant was in command of them or not, and perhaps as a result the attack on the wily Confederate general Sterling Price at Iuka, Mississippi, by Generals Edward O. Ord and Rosecrans, and Rosecrans's defense of Corinth were inconclusive and needlessly bloody battles, productive of very little except casualties. Grant was in the dumps.

Grant was a quick learner but not necessarily a happy one. It is one thing to know how to fight a battle, quite another to learn how to command other generals to fight one, and while he was pleased enough to have Halleck off his back, he had not entirely grown used to handling Halleck's duties as well as his own. Washington expected him to win victories, and that he had done; but now Washington expected him as a military commander to deal with *political* difficulties as well, since he alone represented the United States in what was, practically speaking, enemy territory. Like Ike in North Africa or France, Grant would have to become a politician, an administrator, and a diplomat as well as a general, and none of this came as easily to Grant as fighting did. Not surprisingly he began by putting his foot in it.

It is in the context of this that his notorious General Order #11, expelling Jews from his territory, must be judged. That Grant was enraged by the number of Northern traders who followed his army down the Mississippi, buying up cotton at rock-bottom prices from the defeated Southerners and making fortunes by trading with the enemy, is easy enough to understand—anything to do with trade and money was always an irritant to Grant, to whom the whole subject was a closed book. He was himself not only honest to a fault, but totally hopeless at any kind of business transaction, and the fact that he was now surrounded by people who were good at that kind of thing (and making a fortune out of it) must have been hard for Grant to bear. It did not help that one of them was his own father, Jesse Grant, that astute old rogue, in partnership with a Jewish businessman, or that several members of the Dent family were doing so as well. When Grant lost his temper, it was volcanic and usually short-lived, and General Order #11 was in any case swiftly withdrawn when it reached Lincoln's attention. It has been suggested that Grant's staff, possibly the ubiquitous Rawlins, put into his head the notion that most of the traders he objected to were Jewish, but it seems more likely that Grant suffered from the subliminal anti-Semitism of most American Anglo-Saxons of his day where business affairs were concerned, and that when he lost his temper he attacked the Jews rather than his father and his in-laws—a process we would now call "scapegoating."

Inaction, overwhelming responsibilities for which he was unsuited, and some doubt about what to do next were certainly part of the problem, but worse was to come. Up until then Grant had consoled himself with the thought that he enjoyed Lincoln's confidence, but two events put doubt into Grant's mind. The first was a visit from a well-known and respected newspaperman, Charles A. Dana, whom Edwin Stanton, the secretary of war, had sent to scout out, on Lincoln's behalf, whether there was any truth to the rumors about Grant's drinking that were being spread by his enemies. Dana, as matters would turn out, liked Grant, and his reports to Washington were favorable, but it cannot have eased Grant's nerves to know that he was being watched by somebody who had the ear of both the secretary of war and the president.

The second was the discovery that Lincoln had also been listening hard to Brig. Gen. John A. McClernand, a fellow Illinois politician and amateur general, who proposed to raise a new force of volunteers for the purpose of taking Vicksburg, Mississippi, and had given McClernand secret instructions to proceed.

Vicksburg had long been fitfully on Grant's mind as he sat behind his desk wrestling with such matters as Jewish cotton traders, since it was clear to anybody with a map of the Mississippi at hand that it was the key to opening up the river and splitting the Confederacy. Early in 1862 the navy had seized the city of New Orleans, a serious blow to the Confederacy, but so long as Vicksburg, situated on a high bluff overlooking a sharp bend in the Mississippi, 166 miles north of New Orleans (as the crow flies), remained in Confederate hands, traffic on the river was effectively blocked. Vicksburg had been fortified; it was protected by large numbers of heavy guns and by geography as well, for it was not only on high ground, but the approach from the north was made difficult by the muddy, low-lying swamps of the Yazoo River, which runs sluggishly into the Mississippi.

How McClernand, a mediocre general of volunteers but an astute politician, planned to take Vicksburg is hard to determine, but his greatest weakness was that the secret orders Lincoln had given him contained an escape clause—he was to take on his expedition only those men whom Grant did not need. The threat of McClernand brought Halleck and Grant close again, as thick as thieves, since neither of them wished to have a politician who was a friend of the president's succeed where professional soldiers had failed. Vicksburg suddenly became the focus of Grant's full attention.

This, of course, may have been Lincoln's intention in the first place. Astute politician that he was, he may have been using McClernand to light a fire under Grant as well as to rap him on the knuckles for General Order #11; or he may have felt that two different, competing strategies might be needed to take Vicksburg—except for Winston Churchill in World War II, nobody was more clever at handling generals than Lincoln. Either way, it almost goes without saying that Grant found he needed *all* his troops and could spare none for McClernand, and that by the time McClernand returned to Washington to complain to Lincoln, Grant would already be in Vicksburg.

In the meantime Grant had to get there. Nothing in the history of warfare, including Hannibal's crossing of the Alps with his elephants, has ever posed as much difficulty as Grant's taking of Vicksburg. Like Overlord, the Anglo-American-Canadian D-day landing in 1944, it required huge and startling engineering and technical advances, many of which turned out to be dead ends, and like Anglo-French attempts to break through the German defenses on the western front from 1916 through 1918, it set in motion unprecedented numbers of men through terrain that seemed designed to slow them down and stop them. Mud, rain, flooding, the great river itself—all combined to prevent Grant's men from reaching Vicksburg, and in the end it was only by the boldest and most daring move of his career that he managed to find his way around it to victory. Despite Lee's reputation as a superior strategist, Grant's strategy at Vicksburg was astonishing in its boldness and took advantage of his instinctive understanding of the role of modern industrial technology in warfare—something Lee never even tried to understand.

To take Vicksburg, Grant would use steam shovels, steam dredgers, railways, and steam-powered armored gunboats and turn his army into a giant labor force in which the pick and shovel were more important weapons than the rifle. Grant would eventually have nearly 75,000 men under his command to take Vicksburg, most of them digging and shoveling their way there through the ooze, foot by foot.

Vicksburg sits about two hundred feet above the Mississippi River, on a bluff overlooking the east bank of the river. The Mississippi makes a hairpin bend around Vicksburg, so the batteries of heavy guns dug in around Vicksburg commanded the river itself completely. Adm. David Porter's armored gunboats might survive a determined attempt to slip past the town, but they could do no damage to the Confederate guns, since it was impossible to elevate their own high enough to reach the top of the bluff from the river.

Coming down on Vicksburg by land from the north was rendered impractical by the Yazoo River, which formed an almost impassible swamp as it met the Mississippi. Landing on the east bank, below the Yazoo and just above Vicksburg, at Chickasaw Bluffs, might be possible—at any rate it seemed possible to Sherman when he and Grant looked at the map together, but then most things looked possible to Sherman. In the end it was decided that Sherman would take a part of the army, about 25,000 men, land at Chickasaw Bluffs from Porter's transports, and wait there for Grant, who intended to march the bulk of the army (40,000 plus) inland, move south swiftly, seize Jackson, Mississippi, and then strike west to rendezvous with Sherman.

It is apparent that these plans were not so much aimed at Lt. Gen. John C. Pemberton, the new Confederate commander in Mississippi (with about 32,000 men), as at McClernand, who, in obedience to Lincoln's "secret" plan, was already on the march, and hoped to take command of the Union forces on the river. In any event they miscarried, inevitably, for Grant had committed the classic error of dividing his forces. Grant's position inland was rendered hopeless by a Confederate raid on his supply post; Sherman, unaware that Grant was retreating, attacked at Chickasaw Bluffs and was badly defeated; and McClernand, who had hoped to supplant Sherman, and possibly even Grant, was reduced to impotence by Grant's swift arrival to take personal command of the whole operation.

It was now January 1863. A month had been wasted in maneuvering to the north of Vicksburg, with nothing to show for it but casualties and McClernand's hurt feelings. Clearly Grant would have to *think* his way around Vicksburg.

He looked at the map again and discovered that the Yazoo River had at one time been connected to the Mississippi, and that a levee had been built to separate them and prevent flooding. Cutting the levee might enable Porter to bring his gunboats and transports to the undefended rear of Vicksburg by water. The Confederates, it should be explained, had made the same mistake at Vicksburg that the British did in Singapore eighty years later. Just as the big guns at Singapore had been sited to fire out to sea, thus leaving the city undefended against an attack from the land, the guns at Vicksburg had been placed to defend it from attack from the river or from the north. The "back door" to Vicksburg was lightly defended, and cutting the road or the railway line from Jackson would eventually starve its defenders and inhabitants of supplies.

In the event, the levee was cut, with enormous effort, but the Confederates had had time (and ample warning) to place a fort on high ground and block the gunboats, which had to back their way, under heavy fire, to the Mississippi.

Grant next attempted to descend to the rear of Vicksburg via the bayous, only to find that the Confederates chopped down trees in front of the boats, blocking the way, and then chopped trees down behind them, blocking their retreat, while Confederate sharpshooters picked off anybody who showed his head.

Grant then turned his attention to the west bank of the Mississippi, where the army busied itself building miles of roads and bridges through the marshy ground. It was clear enough that given time and effort they could make their way south of Vicksburg, but what then? The Mississippi was more than half a mile wide, and the troops would need to be transported across it. Grant thought he had a solution to that: He would cut a canal, allowing the fleet to get south of Vicksburg without running the gauntlet of the Confederate batteries on the other side of the river, so the army fell to work to dig a full-scale ship canal, only to have the Mississippi rise and flood it out just as they completed it.

It was now the end of February, and Grant was no nearer Vicksburg than before. In the North the newspapers hurled criticism and ridicule at him, in the South they made fun of him, and McClernand reported back to Washington that Grant was drinking again, which appears to have been untrue. It was, perhaps, his lowest moment as a general, matters not being improved when a steward on his steamer threw Grant's false teeth overboard by mistake. On shore smallpox and cholera were striking the army, due to unsanitary conditions, and in Washington there was talk of replacing Grant. Perplexed and troubled, Lincoln sent Charles A. Dana back again, and once again Dana's reports saved Grant's career and, in some mysterious way, raised Grant's spirits. His dentist, S. L. Hamlin, arrived with a new set of teeth, and Grant sat down at the map again with Porter and Sherman and came up with a new plan.

This one required daring from the navy, but fortunately for Grant, Porter was a kind of seaborne Sherman. Porter would take his fleet down the Mississippi at night past Vicksburg, first his gunboats, then his transports, running the gauntlet of the Confederate guns. Sherman and McClernand, meanwhile, would bring their troops down the west bank of the Mississippi to the aptly named town of Hard Times, where the navy would transport them across the river to Port Gibson, about twenty miles *south* of Vicksburg. Grant would then march the army east and north, probably meet and fight Pemberton, then cut the road and railway between Jackson and Vicksburg. Porter was confident of getting his armored gunboats past Vicksburg but more pessimistic about the fate of the transport steamships, which he proposed to protect with bales of hay and cotton.

It took a long time to organize it all—longest of all to get the army and its vast supplies down to Hard Times on the improvised roads—and it was fortunate that Dana was able to persuade the president to be patient. It would not be until April 16, on a moonless night, which was just what he needed, that Porter was finally able to run his fleet past Vicksburg, and although the Confederates set houses on fire until the river was lit as if by day, and opened up one of the heaviest bombardments of the war, he lost only one transport. In the meantime, on April 17, Grant sent Col. Benjamin H. Grierson off from Memphis, Tennessee, on a cavalry raid that would take Grierson's troopers around Jackson and all the way down to the Union lines at Baton Rouge, Louisiana, diverting Pemberton's attention from what was happening at Hard Times, and revealing the hollowness of the Confederate defenses in Mississippi (the raid would be the subject of *The Horse Soldiers* [1959], a hugely successful movie starring John Wayne as the Grierson character). By April 29 Grant was across the Mississippi with more than 40,000 men, on the same side of the river as Vicksburg and less than twenty miles south of it, while Pemberton, still addled "like a duck hit on the head," to use one of Lincoln's favorite phrases, by the Grierson raid, dithered. He would shortly be reinforced, in numbers if not in determination, by the arrival of Gen. Joseph E. Johnston, with nearly ten thousand men, but in the meantime the damage had been done. Grant would attack Vicksburg by the "back door," while the Confederates wasted time and manpower looking for Grierson's troopers and trying to figure out what they were doing deep behind Confederate lines.

"Don't allow yourself to be shut up in Vicksburg under any circumstances," Johnston had advised Pemberton, but Pemberton eventually did just that. Meanwhile Grant rampaged through Mississippi for three weeks, capturing more than six thousand prisoners, taking more than one hundred guns, and living off the land. At one point he even raided Jefferson Davis's plantation and appropriated one of the Confederate president's favorite horses as his own (he renamed it "Jeff Davis"), revenge perhaps for Davis's snub to Jesse Grant in refusing to reinstate Ulysses' captaincy. In three weeks Grant marched his army two hundred miles, and by the end of May he had cut Pemberton's line of communication with Jackson and effectively trapped him in Vicksburg. On May 22 Grant stormed Vicksburg, taking terrible losses, and was forced to withdraw, the only blessing being that McClernand finally and irrevocably blotted his copybook by his reckless handling of his own troops and his overoptimistic reporting to Grant.

Grant paused to take a deep breath, then invested Vicksburg. If he could not take it by storm, he would starve it out, and so he did. On July 1

Pemberton finally asked for a truce, and on July 3 he and Grant sat down under a tree, Grant smoking a cigar, Pemberton chewing on a blade of grass, to work out the surrender terms.

Grant took nearly 32,000 prisoners and 172 cannon and gave Pemberton more generous terms than he had given Buckner at Fort Donelson, paroling all prisoners until they could be exchanged. Really he had no choice—he had not the time, the place, nor the supplies to deal with them.[1]

TRIUMPHAL ENTRY OF THE UNION ARMY UNDER GENERAL GRANT INTO VICKSBURG, AFTER ITS SURRENDER BY GENERAL PEMBERTON, JULY 4TH, 1863.

Grant's entry into Vicksburg

Right: *Grant meeting General Pemberton*
following the seige of Vicksburg

FRANK LESLIE'S
ILLUSTRATED

NEWSPAPER

Entered according to the Act of Congress in the year 1863, by FRANK LESLIE, in the Clerk's Office of the District Court for the Southern District of New York.

No 410—VOL. XVI.]   NEW YORK, AUGUST 8, 1863.   [PRICE 8 CENTS.

SURRENDER OF VICKSBURG.

Grant's Interview with Pemberton.

It has been Grant's good fortune to appear as the prominent figure in two of the three great surrenders which the rebels have been forced to make—Fort Donelson and Vicksburg.

On the 3d of July a flag of truce came into his lines brought by Major-Gen. Bowen and Col. Montgomery, with a letter from Pemberton, asking a cessation of hostilities in order to arrange terms for the surrender. Grant's characteristic reply was that his only terms were unconditional surrender. Pemberton then asked an interview, which took place at three o'clock, and the surrender was agreed upon.

The next morning Gen. Grant and his Staff met Gen. Pemberton, attended by Col. Montgomery and other officers, at the Stone House inside the rebel works, and Grant formally took possession.

The Slaves of Jefferson Davis coming on to the Camp at Vicksburg.

Few incidents have been more curious and instructive than that witnessed some time before the fall of Vicksburg, when the slaves of Jefferson Davis from his plantation on the Mississippi came into camp. It seemed in itself the doom of slavery, and formed such a contrast to the vaunt of Toombs, that he would call the roll of his slaves on Bunker Hill, that none can help being struck by it. The President of the Confederate States may call the roll of his slaves at Richmond, at Natchez, or at Niagara, but the answer will not come.

Coonskin's Observatory.

None of the sharpshooters in Grant's army has gained a more enviable reputation than Lieut. Foster, of the 23 Indiana, who erected the observatory we portray. He is the California Joe of the West. For a time, having given his cap to another officer, he wore a raccoonskin cap, and as his death-dealing rifle had made the rebels perfectly acquainted with him, they were always on the lookout for Coonskin, whose presence foreboded a speedy close of some rebel's career. His observatory overlooked the rebel works, and commanded some of their guns, so as to render it impossible to use them.

GALLANT CHARGE OF THE 6TH MICHIGAN CAVALRY

At Falling Waters, July 6.

Within the last year our cavalry has risen rapidly in efficiency, and is now, by the admission of rebel officers, far superior to theirs. The superiority of the Southern men as riders, and as cavalry, has proved as baseless as their claim to be descended from the cavaliers of England. The exploits of our cavalry in Virginia, Maryland and Pennsylvania this year would fill a volume in themselves, and rebel soldiers fly at the approach of the Northern troops more fleetly than our men ever did before the redoubtable Black Horse. Yet among the many gallant charges there are few more brilliant than that of the 6th Michigan at Falling Waters, where they rode without drawing rein right over the rebel breastworks, scattering all before them. The cavalry were not more than 50 or 60 at most, but they charged up a steep hill in the face of a terrible fire, and though they lost in killed and wounded nearly two-thirds their number, captured almost the entire force of the enemy, with three regimental battle flags.

MENDELL'S REGULAR ENGINEERS BUILDING A BRIDGE.

The Engineer service seems less brilliant than some other branches of service, and the men a kind of half soldier, half artisan. Yet when bridges are to be built, roads laid, mines run, all look to the engineer. The regular engineers work with great celerity, and in the present sketch we have so incident of Meade's pursuit of Lee, a bridge rapidly thrown over the Antietam, near Funkstown, by a body of regular engineers under Capt. Mendell, on July 11.

MORGAN'S RAID INTO INDIANA—DESTRUCTION OF DEPOT AT SALEM.

Morgan's career of plunder, rapine and destruction seems about to close. His daring invasion of Indiana drew such a force around him that his main body was forced to surrender, while he, true to his gamester antecedents, during the negotiations started off, avoiding a surrender proposed by himself.

SIEGE OF VICKSBURG—GENERAL GRANT MEETING THE REBEL GENERAL PEMBERTON AT THE STONE HOUSE INSIDE THE REBEL WORKS, ON THE MORNING OF JULY 4.—FROM A SKETCH BY OUR SPECIAL ARTIST, FRED. B. SCHELL.

The news reached Washington on July 4, the same day as the news of Pickett's disastrous charge on the last day of Gettysburg. Although Gettysburg, with its fifty thousand casualties, has achieved a place of mythic significance in American history, partly due to Lincoln's speech there, Vicksburg was the more decisive victory. To Lincoln's despair, Meade failed to pursue Lee and allowed him to retreat back across the Potomac to safety, while Grant had won a complete victory. "The Father of Waters again goes unvexed to the sea," wrote Lincoln, and it was true. Grant had opened the Mississippi from the north to New Orleans, splitting the Confederacy in two and opening its heartland to attack—it was the biggest victory in the history of America.

Despite yet another fall from a horse, which laid him up for two weeks, Grant was soon joined in Vicksburg by Julia and their children. In their presence he relaxed until October 1863, when Lincoln ordered him to go with all possible speed to Chattanooga, where a Union army was in desperate straits, and take command there.

Grant moved quickly and took in the situation swiftly—General Rosecrans had been badly beaten by Confederate general Braxton Bragg in the bloody Battle of Chickamauga and was now surrounded in Chattanooga, his army demoralized and starving. Grant relieved Rosecrans, replaced him with Maj. Gen. George H. Thomas, opened up a new supply line down the Tennessee River, and, taking personal command, broke the siege of Chattanooga. Waiting only for Sherman to join him, he then moved to attack Bragg's supposedly impregnable positions on Missionary Ridge, and in a brutal uphill frontal attack—no fancy maneuvering here—drove Bragg back and took six thousand Confederate prisoners.

It was another stunning victory, so widely applauded that it seemed almost inevitable, given the nature of American politics, that Grant would be nominated for the presidency by either the Republicans or the Democrats in '64.

In two years of war Grant had not only proved that he knew how to fight and how to command an army, but also that he knew how to beat the enemy. Like Lincoln, he learned on the job and did not let his ego get in the way. Dogged determination, the ability to take a licking and come back fighting, above all the realization that the enemy's difficulties were at least as great as his own, and perhaps greater—the notion that had struck him with such clarity way back in 1861 when he was still an inexperienced colonel of volunteers pursuing Colonel Harris's Confederates through the countryside around the village of Florida, Missouri—all these had finally matured him into that rarest of men, a successful commander.

Grant was flattered at the offers he received, but not tempted, and was by now wise enough to let Lincoln know it. With a sigh of relief, no doubt— for Lincoln wanted a second term as much as any American president—he persuaded Congress to revive the rank of lieutenant general, nominated Grant be the first to receive that rank, and then called him to Washington to put him in command of all the Union armies.

THE HOME OF GENERAL GRANT.

ST. LOUIS COUNTY MO

*The Grant home
in Galena, Illinois*

General Winfield Scott enters Mexico City

The bombardment of Fort Henry, Tennessee

The storming of Fort Donelson, Tennessee, February 15, 1862

The attack on Fort Donelson,
Grant mounted at center

The Storming of Vicksburg

Union ironclads steaming past Vicksburg at night

Map of the assault on Vicksburg

The Battle of Chattanooga,
Grant standing on rock, holding field glasses

The Battle of Lookout Mountain, near Chattanooga

The Battle of Shiloh

The Battle of Cold Harbor

Detail of Grant

"The Peacemakers"—Sherman, Grant, Lincoln, and Admiral Porter, March 1865

Grant, on steps of the McLean house, and his staff on the porch,
raise their hats in salute to Lee after the surrender

General Robert E. Lee signs the
surrender of his army, April 9, 1865

Grant and his generals

*Nellie Grant's wedding
in the White House*

Right: *President Grant
caricatured in* Puck

Grant's Tomb

CHAPTER

7

G rant arrived in Washington on March 8, 1864—the last time he had visited the capital was to try to persuade the War Department that he was not responsible for the theft of one thousand dollars when he had served as a quartermaster during the Mexican War—and quietly checked in at Willard's Hotel, accompanied by his fourteen-year-old son, Fred. The desk clerk was astonished when the man in the dusty, wrinkled, shabby uniform signed the register, "U. S. Grant and son, Galena, Ill." As the news of his presence spread through the hotel, crowds gathered in the lobby to watch Grant, having put his son to bed, come downstairs to smoke a cigar. Then he walked across Lafayette Park to the White House, where the Lincolns were holding a reception. Leaving his battered black slouch hat with a servant, he joined the crowd in the East Room, an awkward, ill-dressed figure, uneasy, as he always was in social situations without Julia to tell him what to do. Lincoln, either because he had been tipped off or because he recognized the new lieutenant general, came over to him, shook Grant's hand, pulled him into the center of the room, and introduced him to Mrs. Lincoln, saying, "Why look, Mother—here is General Grant."[1]

They must have looked like Mutt and Jeff, Grant a stocky, robust five feet seven, Lincoln an awkward, angular six feet four, but they made conversation—easy for Lincoln, the lawyer and professional politician, but hard work for Grant—until the president, having heard the buzz of excitement in the room at the presence of the victor of Fort Donelson, Shiloh, Vicksburg, and Missionary Ridge, persuaded Grant to stand on a couch so people could see him.

The next day Grant received his formal promotion and sat down for his first serious talk with the president. Lincoln made it clear that he did not intend to look over Grant's shoulder, as he had with so many of his previous generals. He would later write to Grant, "The particulars of your plans I neither know or seek to know," a very different approach from the fretful micromanagement by telegraph that Lincoln had inflicted on McClellan, Burnside (who had burst into tears at the thought of his own inadequacy

Grant receiving his commision as lieutenant general from Lincoln

on being told he was to command the Army of the Potomac), and Hooker, and no doubt Lincoln emphasized his belief that Grant should "hold on with a bulldog grip, and chew & choke, as much as possible."

That was Grant's own view of the matter. He had opened up the South, and would shortly send Sherman on his famous march to the sea; in the meantime he intended to hold on to Lee "with a bulldog grip" until Lee's army was defeated in the field. He had no complicated strategy in mind; he did not much care whether he took Richmond or not—he simply calculated that the North had a larger population than the South, that he could therefore afford casualties better than Lee could in the long run, and that the only way to win was to move forward and push Lee back, day by day, inflicting casualties on the Army of Northern Virginia until the South ran out of men to replace them. It was simple, brutal, and would prove to be effective, but it required a general with Grant's grim view of war to make that deadly calculation and see it through to the bitter end. Lee had remarked to Jackson at Fredericksburg, as he watched Burnside's troops make charge after futile charge into a storm of Confederate fire, "It is well that war is so terrible, or we should grow too fond of it," but it is hard to imagine Grant agreeing with him. He had no romantic notions about war and would surely have agreed with Sherman's famous remark, "War is hell." The waving flags, the glint of bayonets through the smoke, the bugle calls and thunder of artillery drowning out the screams of dying men and horses—none of this held anything in the way of an attraction for Grant. The sooner it was over, the better for all concerned, including the Confederates, and the way to end it fast was to kill them in larger quantities than anybody had heretofore contemplated. It was not a prospect that gave him pleasure—indeed it merely deepened his tendency to melancholy—but he did not shrink before it, or at what it would cost in Union lives.

He moved at once to define and consolidate his position. He intended to command the armies of the East and the West from the field, with the

Army of the Potomac, rather than remain in Washington, so he made a grateful Halleck a kind of chief of staff. Grant did not intend to coop himself up in an office or expose himself to visits from importunate members of Congress or officers of the cabinet—Halleck could do all that for him, and do it better, anyway. He quickly made it clear to Meade that despite Grant's own presence in the field, Meade would remain in command of the Army of the Potomac and did his best to convey his confidence in Meade's ability—no easy task, considering Meade's prickly character. In fact, Grant went out of his way not to interfere with Meade, though inevitably the victor of Gettysburg soon became merely a kind of second in command. Meade's prickliness reached a peak when he had a newspaperman he didn't like drummed out of camp wearing a large sign around his neck with the word "Liar!" in bold letters, about par for the course when it came to Meade's sense of public relations—still his competence as a general was never in doubt.

Grant's strategy for winning the war must be seen against the political realities that concerned the president. Draft riots in the North (represented in our day on film in Martin Scorcese's *Gangs of New York*) were violent and widespread. It was inevitable that growing numbers of the working-class poor in Northern big cities took unkindly to the idea of being conscripted into the army as cannon fodder in order to liberate large numbers of Negroes who would work for lower wages than themselves. The situation was exacerbated by a system that permitted those who had enough money to avoid the draft by paying for a substitute to take their place, an inequity that somewhat resembled the way in which the children of the middle class could avoid the draft by going to graduate school during the Vietnam War, one hundred years later.

Grant was aware of all this, and he did not need Lincoln to point out to him that if the pressure on Lee was lack of manpower and supplies, the pressure on *him* was time. After Lee's defeat at Gettysburg, there was no longer any realistic possibility of the South winning the war, but if it dragged on too long in a series of bloody battles with lengthening casualty lists and no end in sight, there was still a chance for Lincoln to lose the election of '64, and even if he did not, there was still a chance for Northern antiwar feeling to become socially divisive (again, think ahead one hundred years to what happened when substantial numbers of Americans lost faith in victory in Vietnam), either of which could produce a compromise peace. Grant would have to fight hard, but he would also have to press forward and finish the enemy off as quickly as possible.

Previous Union attempts had often been aimed at bypassing the Army of Northern Virginia and taking Richmond—McClellan's disastrous 1862 campaign in the Peninsula, when Lee first acquired his reputation as the South's leading general, had been a perfect example of this—but Grant contemplated no fancy footwork or elaborate attempts to outflank Lee. It was not his style.

Grant had in mind a three-pronged attack on the Confederacy, though in the event, only two of the prongs would do serious damage. He would attack Lee frontally, driving him back on Richmond; the odious but politically powerful Maj. Gen. Benjamin Butler, who was already on the James River, to the southeast of Richmond, would advance on Richmond itself; while Sherman would march through Georgia, take Atlanta, then march on to the sea, cutting Richmond (and Lee's army) off from supplies from the west or the south.

Grant's was to be the main effort. Sherman, Grant knew, could be trusted to succeed, and to pursue a draconian policy of destruction along the way of his advance—for it was Sherman's intention to burn and destroy as much as he could on his march. Butler, who had been thwarted again and again in his attacks on Richmond, without seriously inconveniencing Lee, was to make a more determined effort to threaten the town and give Lee at least some reason to fear for what might be happening behind him.

Butler, true to form, failed to deliver, but Grant, for once, was unable to replace him with a more determined or professional commander, or at least one who was less overbearing and brutally pigheaded—Butler was a politician first and a general second, and Grant was no match for him when it came to political influence that in Butler's case went backstairs all the way up to the White House. He tried to fire Butler and replace him with General Smith, his old West Point instructor; he failed. Even his three stars were no match for Butler.

In the first week of May 1864, Grant moved south and crossed the Rapidan River with nearly 120,000 men—an immense force for the day—and plunged into the region that was known then—and has since become famous in military history—as "the Wilderness," an area of about fifteen square miles of scrub forest, heavy, tangled second-growth woods, abandoned farms, steep gullies, meandering creeks, and primitive cart tracks that had been fought over several times before. The gloominess of the place was made more intense by the unburied skeletons of soldiers on both sides who had died in previous battles on this unpromising ground. It was Grant's hope to cross the river, get through the Wilderness as fast as possible, and fight Lee in more open country where he could make full use of his cavalry and artillery, but Lee was too quick for him. He did not attempt to hinder Grant's crossing of the Rapidan, but the moment Grant's columns were in the Wilderness, Lee attacked, with Ewell on the left and A. P. Hill on the right, bringing Longstreet up as fast as possible to attack between them, in the center. Grant's long columns had to be re-formed into three corps, under (from right to left) John Sedgwick, Gouverneur Warren, and Hancock. It took time on both sides to form a coherent line of battle in such broken, thickly wooded country, and Grant's army was quickly pushed back off its main north–south road into the woods, while Lee's army retained control over the roads running through the Wilderness from west to east. A day of bitter fighting took place, during which the dry undergrowth caught fire, burning the wounded to death where they lay—an additional horror in a day of horrors. Despite Lee's reputation for the daring strategic move, it was, as Wellington described Waterloo, "a pounding match," in which both sides simply closed with each other, fired at point-blank range, and charged with the bayonet.

Grant was expecting the unlucky Burnside to march northwest from the James River to support him, but Burnside became lost in the thick woods and did not appear until late in the day. Almost everybody in the Union army expected that Grant would retreat back across the Rapidan after receiving such a severe mauling—certainly McClellan, Burnside, Hooker, and Meade, when they had been in command, would have done so—but Grant ordered another attack at dawn, and the second day turned out to be as bloody as the first. At the end of it the army was ordered to move during the night, not back to the Rapidan as they expected, but instead to swing around Lee's right, moving south toward Spotsylvania Court House.

Lee was momentarily taken by surprise, but he moved his army fast, getting a step ahead of Grant, and was already in front of Spotsylvania while Grant was trying unsuccessfully to move around his right. From May 8 through May 20, Grant pummeled Lee's positions around Spotsylvania in a series of brutal, head-on attacks, always searching for a way to get around Lee's right, with mounting casualties. On May 11 he wrote to Halleck, "I propose to fight it out on this line, if it takes all summer" (another Grant line that was to become famous), and he clearly meant it. As the casualties rose, the old rumors and criticism that had surfaced after Shiloh were raised again—that Grant was drunk, incompetent, "a butcher." Union casualties may have been as high as eighteen thousand—the fighting was so intense that there was no time to count them—and Confederate casualties reached almost twelve thousand, a crippling loss for the Army of Northern Virginia; still the fighting went on with no letup. Grant truly had "a bulldog grip" on Lee.

At last Grant turned Lee's flank, but Lee once more managed to get ahead of him, and the two armies fought day by day, foot by foot, Grant advancing, Lee retreating toward Richmond, until, on June 2, Grant was within six miles of Richmond, with nothing but Lee's dwindling but still considerable army between him and the city. Still, that was enough. Lee was an engineer—his positions were carefully chosen, and protected with formidable breastworks and deep trenches. Grant ordered a full attack for the next day—the day that would see him lose his temper at the Union teamster beating a horse around the head—and by noon, in less than half an hour's fighting, he had lost some seven thousand men without shifting the Confederates an inch from their positions.[2] It was, even in his own eyes, the nadir of his generalship.

The next day even Grant was forced to stop and reconsider, especially since it was by no means sure at this point that the Union troops could, or would, make another charge over ground that was still thickly covered with Union dead and wounded. With one of those swift changes of mind that mark the true military genius, Grant decided to give up the position that had cost him so many lives and cross the James River to the south of Richmond. He would move his army to where Butler had been ineffectually camped, abandon his line of communication to the north, and take up positions where he could be supplied by steamships coming up the James. From there he would move his army to the left in an effort to cut the railway lines running to Richmond from the south, in effect choking Lee off from his supplies.

By June 14 Grant had his army across the James, and he determined at once to move on Petersburg, a small town south of Richmond through which one of the major railways ran. He moved immediately to take Petersburg, but the Confederate forces there, under the command of General Beauregard, with fewer than fifteen thousand men to Grant's fifty thousand, managed to hold out until Lee could disengage from his lines north of Richmond and bring the Army of Northern Virginia by forced march into Petersburg. Grant's generals may have been hesitant to attack after the experience of Cold Harbor, and the men themselves may at that point have been reluctant to attempt another frontal attack, but whatever the reason, the brief moment in which the Union army might have seized Petersburg passed with Lee's arrival on the scene, and both enemies settled down for a long siege.

Grant's view of his position echoed that of Gen. Joseph Joffre fifty years later when he was asked how he proposed to defeat the Germans after they had entrenched themselves following the Battle of the Marne—"*Je les grignote*," Joffre said ("I shall nibble away at them"), and that is precisely what Grant set out to do, with a seemingly endless series of attacks against the Confederate trenchworks from his own, the kind of fighting which was to characterize war on the western front for four long years. Artillery bombardments, mining, bayonet charges, sniping, and hand-to-hand fighting became the defining activities of the siege of Petersburg—those and death by disease as tens of thousands of men huddled together in conditions of primitive unsanitariness.

At City Point, a steamer landing on the south side of the James, Grant built up a whole city of wooden huts, the headquarters and supply base for an army of 125,000 men, and he was soon joined there by Mrs. Grant and their children. Conditions were primitive; mud or dust, depending on the season, was omnipresent; huge quantities of guns, food, forage, and ammunition were accumulated; field hospitals built and staffed—it was in every way the equivalent of a modern army's base of supply, a sight so impressive that visitors could hardly imagine why the war was still going on or how the Confederates were still able to resist, but then, as Grant explained when he was in the mood, Lee had the advantage of interior lines, so that he could quickly reinforce his defending troops anyplace where they were attacked.

Grant, Julia Grant,
and their son Jesse,
City Point, 1864

From time to time Lincoln would come down by steamer to visit Grant, and the two were usually photographed together from a respectful distance, sitting opposite each other glumly under an awning, as if the weight of the world rested on their shoulders, which, in a sense, it did. They look as if they were sitting in complete silence, something that would have been uncommon for Lincoln but not for Grant. Perhaps the best-known photograph of Grant was taken by Mathew Brady at City Point, Grant leaning against a tree in front of a tent, his uniform wrinkled and dusty, his hat pushed back a bit on his head, his eyes, at once determined and deeply sad, staring into the far distance over the photographer's shoulder. He is not elegantly turned out, his trousers and shoes are muddy, but he is *not* wearing a private's uniform—simply a dark blue suit with a long frock coat and a waistcoat, decked out with gilt buttons and the shoulder bars of a three-star general. He looks careworn and miserably unhappy, as he surely was, and perhaps in need of a stiff drink.

Grant in 1864

In July he made two attempts to move things forward. One was to send Sheridan on a long ride behind the enemy lines, which proved how little there was in the way of armed forces behind Lee, and in which he ravaged the Shenandoah Valley on the way home; the other was to employ former mining engineers to tunnel under the Confederate lines and explode a tremendous mine—the biggest in the history of warfare to that date. It went off with an enormous explosion on July 30, killing two hundred Confederate soldiers and creating a huge crater, but the Union troops who rushed into it, disorganized and poorly led, soon found themselves trapped in the crater, with the Confederates shooting down into it, like "shooting fish in a barrel," as one survivor said. By the time it was over, Grant had lost almost four thousand men for no gain—just the kind of thing that would happen again and again on the western front in World War I, proving, perhaps, that instructors in staff colleges the world over are usually several wars behind. In retaliation for Sheridan's raid, Confederate general Jubal A. Early raided deep into Maryland, nearly took Washington, D.C., by surprise, then retreated home again, burning down the city of Chambersburg, Pennsylvania, on the way. Grant and Lincoln had plenty to be glum about.

The summer limped on into autumn, then winter, while day after day men died in the lines around Petersburg; then, quite suddenly, at the beginning of April 1865, Lee's forces were finally obliged to retreat—they no longer had the strength to hold Richmond. On April 2 Jefferson Davis abandoned the capital of the Confederacy, while Lee and what remained of the Army of Northern Virginia retreated toward Lynchburg, Virginia. Lee still cherished a notion to retreat south, join forces with Gen. Joseph E. Johnston's army in North Carolina, defeat Sherman, then march back north to attack Grant, but events rapidly made any such plan impossible, as Grant's armies took one by one the roads and railways that would have made the move feasible.

Grant had kept "a bulldog" grip on Lee for nearly eight months, while

Sherman's army, and others, destroyed or burned railways, bridges, whole cities like Atlanta, crops, barns, and proud homes all over the Confederacy, and "freed" the slaves as well, in the sense at least of turning them loose on the roads and depriving their former owners of the capital that a slave represented. Confederate money was worthless paper, the Confederate capital was looted and burnt to the ground, Confederate illusions were shattered, the Confederacy itself was effectively reduced to Lee and his army—weakened, starving, but still dangerous, retreating by muddy back roads into the Virginia countryside, perhaps to make a last stand.

It is with that in mind that one must read Grant's letter to Lee, surely one of the most dignified in the history of war. He and Meade had harried and surrounded Lee's army, while the bumptious Custer had destroyed much of Lee's supply train, but the one thing Grant did not want was a heroic finale to the war.

Headquarters Armies of the U. S.

5 P. M., April 7, 1865
General R. E. Lee
Commanding C. S. A.

The results of the last week must convince you of the hopelessness of further resistance on the part of the Army of Northern Virginia in this struggle. I feel that it is so, and regard it as my duty to shift from myself the responsibility of any further effusion of blood, by asking of you the surrender of that portion of the Confederate States army known as the Army of Northern Virginia.

U. S. Grant
Lieut.-General.

Lee replied the same evening with a short but equally gracious reply. While "not entertaining the opinion you express on the hopelessness of further resistance," Lee reciprocated Grant's "desire to avoid a useless effusion of blood," and asked for his terms of surrender.

This was not good enough for Grant, but it opened the door a crack to peace. He wrote back to Lee the next morning that he would accept Lee's surrender of his army on "one condition, namely that the men and officers surrendered shall be disqualified from taking up arms again against the Government of the United States until properly exchanged," and proposed that Lee should choose a time and place for a meeting. These were approximately the same terms he had offered Pemberton at Vicksburg, and a lot better than his famous "unconditional surrender" letter to Buckner. But then Buckner was not Lee, for whom Grant felt a great respect.

Both armies were still moving west as the two generals communicated, Lee's slowly and painfully, Grant's more quickly, while Grant tried to separate Lee from the South. On the morning of the ninth, the head of Lee's column reached Appomattox Station, only to find Custer's troopers already in possession of it, and the supplies waiting there. In the meantime Grant was suffering, as he often did when under stress, from a severe migraine headache. He took refuge in a farmhouse and spent the night of the eighth bathing his feet "in hot water and mustard" and applying "mustard plasters" to his wrists and neck.

The early morning of the ninth brought another, longer letter from Lee, implying that he understood Grant's terms but still not specifically agreeing to them. It was a step in the right direction, however, and it got Grant out of his sickbed and onto his horse. Severe fighting had resumed, and although Appomattox Court House was only two or three miles away as the crow flies, there was no way for Grant to ride through it. Lee sent messengers under the white flag of truce to Meade and to Sheridan, asking for "a suspension of hostilities" to allow for a meeting between himself and Grant. Meade set a time limit of two hours, and Grant rode south with a modest escort, to get around the area where the fighting had been taking place, then turned north and reached Appomattox Court House by the back roads, his head still pounding. On the way he received yet another note from Lee, borne by a Confederate officer, at last agreeing to Grant's terms, and Grant's headache instantly vanished. He quickly scrawled a reply to Lee from horseback, saying that he was "four miles West of Walker's Church," and asking for an officer to conduct him to where Lee was, and after a long and confusing ride on muddy country roads was led to the McLean house in the village of Appomattox Court House, where Lee was waiting for him. Reading between the lines, it seems likely that Grant plunged off into the Virginia countryside and got lost, something it is possible to do even today in a car, with a map in hand. What is also worth noting is that it took a high degree of courage for a three-star general to ride through back roads where it was only too likely he would meet angry Confederate soldiers, any one of whom might be only too happy to kill the Union commander—a thought that does not even seem to have occurred to Grant.

He arrived slightly embarrassed by his muddy uniform, particularly since

The McLean house, Appomattox Court House, Virginia

Lee was waiting for him on the porch of the McLean house in a brand-new, beautifully tailored pale gray uniform, gold braid glistening on his sleeves, a scarlet sash and a gold-braided belt around his waist, wearing a gilt presentation sword (probably the one presented to him by the state of Virginia), and carrying his white kidskin riding gloves in one hand, every inch the patrician *beau sabreur* of legend. He stood erect, six feet tall, with gleaming boots, a perfectly trimmed white beard, and the piercing eyes of a born commander of men, a figure of awesome military dignity, as Grant clumped up the steps in his muddy boots and wrinkled uniform to meet him. As Grant commented with undisguised admiration, "What General Lee's feelings were I do not know. As he was a man of much dignity, with an impassible [*sic*] face, it was impossible to say whether he felt inwardly glad that the end had finally come, or felt sad over the result, and was too manly to show it."

Despite the best efforts of Lee's staff, and of Grant's, things were not quite ready for the two commanders in the small, cramped house, and they stood making small talk for a few minutes, mostly about the Mexican War. Grant remembered Lee well, and Lee at any rate pretended to remember Grant, despite the fact that they had been separated by a great distance of age and rank, and they chatted together so pleasantly about old campaigns and old army friends that Lee finally had to remind Grant what they were there for.

Once they were inside—Lee raised a well-bred eyebrow at Col. Ely Parker, Grant's full-blooded Indian staff officer—they sat down together at a small table, and Lee suggested that Grant put the terms he was suggesting in writing. Parker hunted up paper, an inkwell, and a pen, and Grant scratched away while Lee politely stared at the walls. On his own it occurred to Grant to put in a sentence allowing Confederate officers to retain their sidearms, private horses, and baggage, to "avoid unnecessary humiliation."

No conversation took place until Grant passed the letter to Lee, who put on his reading glasses and perused it carefully. When he came to the part about officers retaining their sidearms, horses, and baggage, he remarked, "with some feeling," Grant thought, that this would have "a happy effect" upon his army.

Lee raised only one point, which was that in the Confederate army cavalrymen and "artillerists" owned their own horses, and asked if they would be permitted to retain them. Grant pointed out that the exemption was for officers only, and that he could not or would not rewrite his letter, but since most of the men were small farmers, and would need to plant their crops, his officers would be instructed to allow any Confederate soldier who claimed a horse or a mule to take the animal to his home. Lee remarked again that this would have "a most happy effect," and, taking a piece of paper, wrote out his acceptance of the terms in five brief lines.

While the exchange of letters was being copied, Lee and Grant chatted quietly, filling in time. Lee, in the end, did not offer Grant his sword, nor would Grant, in view of the line he had written into the surrender terms, have accepted it. Lee did point out, with some embarrassment, that his troops were starving, and Grant agreed to provide him rations for 25,000 men. With that they parted, perhaps the most famous scene in American history having been completed in less than an hour, and Grant wrote out a few lines to be telegraphed to Stanton with perhaps the least self-congratulatory or exultant message of victory in the history of warfare:

Headquarters Appomattox C. H., Va.,

April 9th, 1865, 4:30 P. M.
Hon. E. M. Stanton, Secretary of War,
Washington.

General Lee surrendered the Army of Northern Virginia this afternoon on terms proposed by myself. The accompanying additional correspondence will show the conditions fully.

U. S. Grant,
Lieut.-General.

As the news spread through the Union lines, the Union artillery began to fire a one-hundred-gun salute. Grant, whose headache was returning, sent word to have it stopped. Whether he actually said "We are all Americans again now" is doubtful, but that was certainly his thought. "The Confederates," he later wrote, "were now our prisoners, and we did not want to exult over their downfall."

What he thought about the story that Custer, the "boy general," had ridden off from the McLean house with the small table on which the surrender had been signed held upside down on his head, taking it away as a souvenir, we do not know, but it may well have been one of the many reasons for his dislike of Custer, whose death at the Little Big Horn Grant took with something that goes well beyond stoicism, approaching a certain satisfaction. In any event the next day he permitted his officers to visit any friends they might have in the Confederate camp (the professional army

was a small world), and he himself rode over to the McLean house again for a long and friendly chat with Lee. Lee gracefully declined to issue a call for the remaining Confederate armies to surrender, saying that he could not do so without consulting his president, and the two men shook hands and parted, Lee to return to his defeated army, Grant to proceed by railway to Washington, where, he felt, his presence was urgently required.

For all practical purposes the Civil War was over. Grant was forty-three years old.

The New-York Times.

VOL. XIV.....NO. 4220.   NEW-YORK, TUESDAY, APRIL 4, 1865.   PRICE FOUR CENTS

GRANT.

RICHMOND

AND

VICTORY!

The Union Army in the Rebel Capital.

Rout and Flight of the Great Rebel Army from Richmond.

Jeff. Davis and His Crew Driven Out.

Grant in Close Pursuit of Lee's Routed Forces.

Richmond and Petersburgh in Full Possession of Our Forces.

ENTHUSIASM IN THE REBEL CAPITAL.

The Citizens Welcome Our Army with Demonstrations of Joy.

RICHMOND FIRED BY THE ENEMY

Our Troops Save the City from Destruction.

THE EVACUATION OF PETERSBURGH.

FIRST DISPATCH.

[OFFICIAL.]

War Department,
Washington, April 3—10 P. M. }

To Major-Gen. Dix:

The following telegram from the President, announcing the EVACUATION OF PETERSBURGH and probably of Richmond, has just been received by this department.

EDWIN M. STANTON, *Secretary of War.*

City Point, Va., April 3—8:30 A. M. }

To Hon. Edwin M. Stanton, Secretary of War:

This morning Lieut. Gen. GRANT reports Petersburgh evacuated, and he is confident that Richmond also is.

He is pushing forward to cut off, if possible, the retreating rebel army.

A. LINCOLN.

THE CAPTURE OF RICHMOND.

SECOND DISPATCH.

War Department, Washington, D. C. }

To Maj.-Gen. Dix:

[Continued on Eighth Page.]

THE GLORIOUS NEWS.

Rejoicings in City and Country

Enthusiasm, Solemnity and Thanksgiving.

Business Suspended and Flags Displayed.

The Praise of the Army on Every Tongue.

Great Mass Meetings in Wall Street and at Union Square.

Patriotic Speeches and Patriotic Songs.

The Whole City Aglow with Excitement.

ILLUMINATIONS AND FIREWORKS.

A GALLERY OF

Political Cartoons

FROM THE YEARS OF

GRANT'S PRESIDENCY

THE NARROW PATH.

ALEX. STEVENS.—" *Come, Jeff, let's go over, I don't like this side of the ditch.*"
JEFF. DAVIES.— "*don't like it any better than you do, but I don't like to say so, and if they'd only make the gangway a little wider I think I'd go. Why don't they put down that State Rights' plank, and the ....*"
FATHER ABRAHAM.— "*Narrow as the path is, it is the only way in which you can come over ; and you will have to come soon, for I perceive there are two fellows behind you that will leave you nothing but the inside of the ditch, where so many of your friends agreed to meet, if you don't hurry up.*"

THE PRECARIOUS SITUATION.

THE MODERN GULLIVER AMONG THE LILLIPUTIANS.

WIPING OUT STATE LINES.

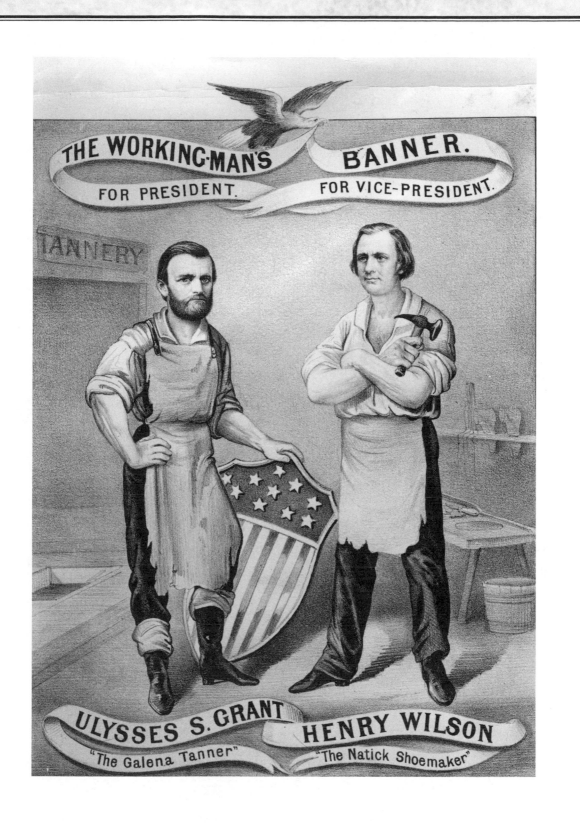

REPUBLICAN PLATFORM,
OR THE POLITICAL MOUNTEBANK.

AN IMPENDING CATASTROPHE.

Published by Currier & Ives, 152 Nassau St. N.Y.

Platform

Grant

PLATFORM

1868?

INDICTMENT OF GULLIVER GRANT.

"They insist that you shall be put to the most painful and ignominious death."

[Gulliver, after conquering the forces of Blefuscu, and restoring peace to Lilliput, was waited upon by one of the Lilliputians, who told him that his doom was sealed.]

THE NATIONAL GRAB-BAG.

FARMER—"*I can't make a living out of this animal any longer; but I must keep my end up. You must let loose.*"
RAILROAD PRESIDENT—"*Well, I can't declare any dividends; but I must keep head and tail of the thing.*"
ULYSSES—"*But I've got a good thing of it, and I'll* GRAB *till she's stripped.*"

CALLING IN FRAUDS.

"Step up, Gentlemen. (?) Don't be Bashful!"

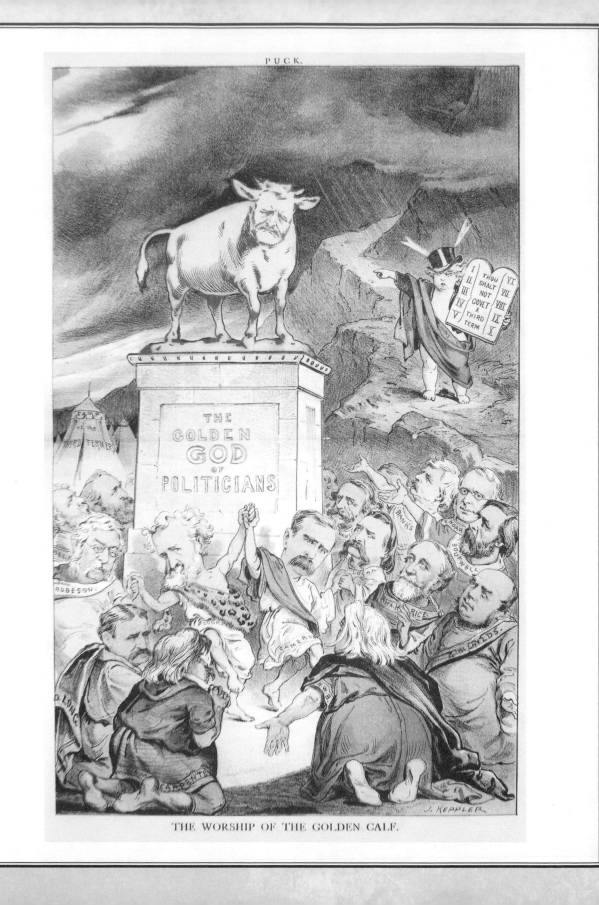

THE WORSHIP OF THE GOLDEN CALF.

VOL. IX.—No. 223. JUNE 15, 1881. Price, 10 Cents.

"What fools these Mortals be!"
MIDSUMMER-NIGHTS DREAM

Puck

PUBLISHED BY
KEPPLER & SCHWARZMANN.
NEW YORK
TRADE MARK REGISTERED 1878
OFFICE No. 21—23 WARREN ST.

ENTERED AT THE POST OFFICE AT NEW YORK, AND ADMITTED FOR TRANSMISSION THROUGH THE MAILS AT SECOND CLASS RATES."

GRANT AS HIS OWN ICONOCLAST.

UNCONDITIONAL SURRENDER.

U. S. GRANT—"*It is not for myself that I grieve—but what will become of my poor relations?*"

CHAPTER

8

Many biographers of Grant have suggested that his career after Appomattox was driven mainly by a need to keep busy and for applause. Doubtless there is some truth to that—Grant, as his own mother would point out, had become a great man while he was still young, and neither he nor Julia contemplated a retreat to Galena for the rest of their lives, even though the good citizens of Galena would shortly present the Grants with a house worth sixteen thousand dollars, a tidy sum for the day, completely furnished, right down to the leather-bound sets of books in the library and the pictures on the walls. Still, one must also consider his inflexible sense of duty. The presidency was something he could not avoid.

Had Mrs. Grant not raised objections to the invitation to accompany the Lincolns to the theater—an invitation Grant had as good as accepted, and that he was then obliged to decline with considerable embarrassment—Grant might have been shot by John Wilkes Booth along with President Lincoln. Mrs. Grant made such a fuss over the prospect of another ghastly evening of being snubbed by Mary Lincoln—who had loudly objected to Julia's remaining seated while she, the president's wife, stood, on a visit to City Point, and then made an even worse scene about Major General Ord's wife's hat—that poor Grant had to fumble around with lame excuses, the lameness of which must have been quite obvious to Lincoln, and was therefore spared being present when Lincoln was shot. Even twenty years later, when he wrote his memoirs, Grant was still concocting new and unconvincing explanations for why the Grants had been obliged to stand the Lincolns up at the last moment.

As soon as he heard the news of the assassination, Grant moved quickly to have Ford, the owner of the theater, arrested by Ord, then settled down to the more than ample work of the commanding general of the army. He would shortly be honored by becoming the first American officer since George Washington to be made a full four-star general.

It explains much about Grant if one compares him to a later general, Dwight D. Eisenhower. Like Eisenhower, Grant was perceived as "a man of the people"; like Eisenhower, his conduct of the war was universally admired; and like Eisenhower, though he was no politician, he could obviously have the presidency when he wanted it—in fact, would be sought for the presidency by both parties whether he wanted it or not. Crowds waited to see Grant trot to the office every morning in Washington, driving himself at a spanking pace, reins in his hands while smoking his trademark cigar, and politicians sought his advice—or at least his presence—at every discussion of national policy. Grant was not just popular, in the vacuum that followed the assassination of President Lincoln, he was one of the major figures, perhaps *the* major figure, to give the administration of Andrew Johnson authority and *gravitas*—both qualities the new president conspicuously lacked himself.

Part of Grant's authority derived from his silence. In a world in which politicians spoke for hours (the speech preceding Lincoln's address at Gettysburg ran longer than two hours, and most of the audience thought it was too short), Grant's reluctance to speak at all seemed like proof of his wisdom. People listened carefully to what he *did* have to say—like the utterances of the Sphinx—puzzled over his meaning, and interpreted his silences as a sign of greatness. In an age when speechmaking was a popular entertainment (the term "stemwinder" comes from a speech so long that listeners had to rewind their watch during its course), and when folksy, comic, and sometimes bawdy stories were political assets (Lincoln was the past master of these), Grant had neither a gift nor a taste for either one. Way back when he had been chosen to command a regiment of volunteers by the governor of Illinois, he had listened to other people's full-blown rhetoric as they addressed the troops; then, when it was his turn, stood before his new men, who were no doubt expecting still more rhetoric, and said, "Go to your quarters, men."

They had admired him for that, and his gift for brevity had encouraged and rallied troops at Fort Donelson, Shiloh, and elsewhere during the war. It mystified politicians, however, who assumed that Grant's taciturnity was a way of hiding his opinions, although Julia could have taught them otherwise. Grant's taciturnity was natural and unaffected. He was a good listener who liked to think things over before speaking his mind, and arrived at his conclusions by some silent, interior process known only to himself.

Grant, like Wellington after Waterloo, soon became a major "fixer" of seemingly insoluble problems, the one man who could be trusted to deal calmly, quietly, authoritatively, and above all *fairly* with matters that had everyone else in Washington stumped. He was not a party man as such, though he thought of himself as a Republican because of his admiration for Lincoln (his memoirs are nonetheless singularly lacking in emotion on the subject of Lincoln's death), and for a time a part of his strength was that he was perceived to be above party loyalty and, more important, above party intrigue. He was trusted in the South as well as the North, which gave him a special position at a time when the burning question of the day was how to reintegrate the Southern states into the union, and on what terms.

From the very first he was uncomfortable with President Johnson, a former tailor and Democrat who talked too much, was inappropriately quarrelsome with any stranger who expressed disagreement with him, and was prone to act rashly. These failings were exacerbated by the rumor that Johnson was a drunk, which may have come about because of an unfortunate incident. Johnson had been about to address the Congress, and complained of a severe attack of diarrhea—a real problem in a day when speeches were expected to go on for hours. A well-meaning senator advised a stiff shot of brandy to steady the president's bowels, and Johnson, who was unused to strong drink, followed his advice and as a result made a rambling, inarticulate speech, following which he had to be helped off the podium.

The rumor that the new president had been drunk when he addressed the House and Senate did nothing for Johnson's popularity—though even without that it would have been hard to follow the martyred Lincoln into the presidency—but at the nub of the problem was Johnson's view of making peace with the South. Although he was a border state man (which was the reason he had been chosen for the vice presidency in the first place), unlike Lincoln, Johnson wanted Southerners to be punished for rebellion and treason and was determined to take a hard line. This put him at odds with Grant, who, like Lincoln, did not want to see former Confederates punished merely for their opinions, as opposed to what we would now call genuine war crimes, and was reluctant to lend his prestige to attempts on the part of the president to coerce the Southern states. Johnson's misfortune, however, was that the radical wing of his party wanted him to go even further than he was willing to in punishing the South, so he was caught between a rock and a hard place.

One of Grant's first tasks was to censure his old friend Sherman, who, in accepting the surrender of Joseph E. Johnston in North Carolina, had wildly and impulsively exceeded his authority with a document that allowed Confederate forces to take their arms home and deposit them in state arsenals, recognized existing state governments, and confirmed "property rights" without defining them, so that there was a possibility that the courts might hold them to include former slaves. What was going on in Sherman's mind is hard to say—he was recklessly impulsive and prone to touches of megalomania—but Grant was obliged to write him a stiff letter and to repudiate the surrender agreement, then travel by train across the stricken South to take command of Sherman's army and renegotiate the terms of Johnston's surrender.

By the time Grant returned to Washington, President Johnson was already deeply enmeshed in the struggle with Congress over Reconstruction legislation that would end in his impeachment proceedings. In the summer of 1866, Johnson had taken what we would now call a whistle-stop tour of the Northern states to drum up support for his policies, and ordered Grant to accompany him as window dressing. To Grant's embarrassment, the tour was a disaster, and even his presence in uniform was insufficient to calm audiences, as they and the president exchanged insults and threats.

By the winter of 1866, fueled by the failure of Johnson's tour, Congress was busy drafting legislation designed to hog-tie the president hand and foot to the extreme Radical cause—military government was to be imposed on the Southern states, the president was to be enjoined from issuing any orders to the army except through the general in command, and to be forbidden from dismissing any member of his cabinet without the consent of the Senate.

Grant's views on Reconstruction were complicated—or at any rate contradictory—but he was, above all, not an extremist. He disliked the idea of dividing the South into military districts, but would obey orders, and he was no great enthusiast for attempts "to enfranchise the Negro, in all his ignorance," though in that too he would obey orders. Above all he

did not want to get drawn into the quarrel that was fast developing between the president and the Radical members of his own cabinet, and
between the president and Congress. Inexorably, however, he was drawn
into the struggle, when Johnson removed Stanton as secretary of war and
appointed Grant temporarily in his place. When the Senate set aside the
president's action, Grant obligingly moved out of the office of secretary of
war and let Stanton reassume it, thus inviting Johnson's rage. Johnson
thenceforth regarded Grant as having betrayed him, while Grant regarded
Johnson as having insulted him.

The turmoil of Reconstruction led finally to Johnson's impeachment,
which he narrowly survived—no thanks to Grant—but which spelled the
end of his political career. In May 1868 Grant was nominated unanimously
as the Republican candidate for the presidency.

Campaign poster

Sheet music cover, Grant campaign song

*Grant accepts
the nomination*

He went "home" to his new house in Galena and won the election without making any speeches or a campaign tour or even appearing much in public in Galena. He could be seen from time to time taking a constitutional stroll or a drive, or seated on the porch smoking a cigar, but that was as much as he would contribute to the electoral process, and as much as was needed.

He created something of a stir by refusing to ride in the same carriage as Andrew Johnson on inauguration day, but his failure to campaign and his short and notably bland inauguration speech left most people in some doubt as to what his policies would be—doubt that was shared to a sig-

Grant's first inaugural

nificant degree by Grant himself. Almost seventy years later the outgoing president, Harry Truman, would remark of Eisenhower that he would never know what hit him when he reached his desk in the White House—as a general, when he gave an order it would be obeyed instantly, but in the White House he would give an order and nothing would happen. The same phenomenon hit Grant almost immediately. He too, like Ike, was accustomed to instant obedience, not to the political process of building up support for a policy in Congress, or appealing for support to the public, or wooing newspapermen to obtain it. He expected at the very least the backing of his own party, without realizing that everything in politics has to be negotiated—at a price.

Grant's presidency has come in for a good deal of criticism, and it is certainly true that it ended badly in financial and political scandals, but the fact remains that for eight years Grant exerted a calming influence on a country that had only just emerged from a bloody civil war. (Nearly 625,000 Americans had been killed in the war—compare this with 400,000 in World War II and 58,000 in Vietnam, in a country with four or five times the population it had in the mid–nineteenth century—and a large part of the country remained devastated, starving, and sunk in catastrophic defeat.) Grant not only managed to bring the South back into the Union, albeit at a price the Radicals did not want to pay, and with racial problems that would continue to plague the United States a hundred years later, but also managed to avoid foreign wars or entanglements. Grant's sheer presence, like Ike's eighty years later, his immense prestige, his "unflappability" (as someone would describe the supposed salient characteristic of the British prime minister from 1957 to 1963, Harold Macmillan), more or less guaranteed that the United States would be taken seriously again by the world's great powers. Lincoln, with his death, reached, like Gandhi, an international sainthood, but Grant, like Ike, was the symbol of something else: America's military power, the integrity of its institutions, its basic decency and good intentions, and above all its rock-solid common sense.

Michael Korda

Nobody thought Grant would be much good at diplomacy (wrongly), or politics and policy making (which turned out to be true), but his person, his character, his rise from the leather and harness shop in Galena to four-star general and president, confirmed something much larger—the American dream. No other American of the nineteenth century attained such fame and worldwide admiration, not even Lincoln, whose saintly martyrdom and political cunning made him much harder to understand than the bluff, solid Grant.

Pictures of the Grants in the White House do not make it seem as if they enjoyed themselves there. Grant, in civilian clothes, looks rumpled, uncomfortable, and top-heavy, and seems to have put on a good deal of weight (as did Mrs. Grant), and in a magazine illustration of Chief Red Cloud's visit to a White House reception, Red Cloud and his followers in their blankets and feathers look more elegant and more at ease than their hosts, the Grants. Grant has been criticized for his choice of cabinet officers, but in the nineteenth century as it is today it was considered perfectly acceptable to reward one's friends with a cabinet post, so it is hardly surprising that Elihu Washburne, the representative who had picked Grant to command the Galena volunteers, was made secretary of state briefly, then American minister to France. Other choices ranged from the banal to the incomprehensible, also very much as they do today, but the selection of Hamilton Fish to replace Washburne as secretary of state was a fortunate one, as was that of former Ohio governor and Civil War general Jacob D. Cox for the Department of the Interior and Grant's old aide John A. Rawlins as secretary of war. Grant was widely criticized for giving his relatives jobs, but that is an old Anglo-American political tradition, and most of the jobs were small potatoes indeed. To please Julia Grant, one supposes, her brother became a government Indian trader in New Mexico, another brother was appointed a minor customs official in San Francisco, while a second cousin of hers became receiver of public moneys in Oregon. Her brother Frederick became Grant's appointments secretary in the White House, while her father (already a postmaster, thanks to Andrew Jackson) moved into the White House as a kind of permanent houseguest, waylaying strangers in the halls to describe the glories of the Confederacy and the inadequacies of the Negro race. As these things go, or went, it was not nepotism on any grand scale.

Grant and his cabinet

Grant's grasp of foreign affairs, perhaps due to the help of Hamilton Fish, was better than anybody could have wished. Like most successful generals, his first concern was peace. A burning issue of the day was the fact that the *parvenu* emperor of France, Napoleon III, nephew of the great Napoleon, had conspired to evade the Monroe Doctrine by putting an Austrian Hapsburg archduke on the hastily improvised throne of Mexico during the Civil War, an idea he hoped would please the Austrians at no great expense to France. This bizarre episode of what would now be called neocolonialism was bitterly opposed by most Mexicans and also deeply resented by Americans. With the end of the Civil War, the United States had available what was arguably the largest, best armed, and most experienced army in the world, and there were many who thought it should be used to invade Mexico and drive the French out. Grant himself had toyed with the idea ("On to Mexico!" he is said to have remarked facetiously when the Civil War ended), but as president he used his best efforts to calm things down between the United States and France, emphasizing that France was America's first and oldest ally and friend (a sentiment that might usefully have been followed 133 years later by President George W. Bush), and that Napoleon III would doubtless vanish from the scene without American help, which is exactly what happened. The unfortunate Emperor Maximilian of Mexico was executed by a Mexican firing squad, Napoleon III abdicated his throne in 1870 after having been defeated in the field by the Prussians, and the United States avoided the perils of intervention in Mexico and the risk of war with France. Had it existed then, Grant would have deserved the Nobel Peace Prize.

There were other, thornier problems, however, and these Grant failed to grasp. The line the Clinton people threw at George Bush *père* in the 1992 election campaign might have been aimed with equal effect at Grant: "It's the economy, stupid." It was Grant's misfortune that he had no business sense whatsoever in an age when the economy was rapidly becoming the major issue. After the Civil War the United States was saddled with a huge national debt, the South's economy was virtually destroyed, the West was being opened up at a rapid pace (despite the increasingly desperate resistance of those whom Grant called "the original occupants of this land"), and industrialization would very shortly make U.S. productivity soar above that of the United Kingdom. New inventions small and large were changing American life at a dizzying pace: the telegraph, the vast expansion of the railroads, gaslight, the iron-hulled, steam-engined ocean liner and battleship, new agricultural machinery, the safety razor, the repeating rifle, the fountain pen—there seemed no end to American invention and ingenuity—while at the same time the cities of the Northeast and Midwest expanded at breakneck speed to accommodate millions of new immigrants, creating a building boom and sending land prices sky-high.

All these things required vast amounts of capital—capital on an unprecedented scale—and Wall Street, with its speculators, financiers, merchant bankers, and stockbrokers, became a power in the land, perhaps, some feared, *the* power in the land. Jeffersonian democracy, the ideal of the small farmer and the sturdy local merchant—all of that was about to be overwhelmed as surely as the tribes of "hostile" Indians west of the Missouri River. On the subject of the Indians, Grant's sympathies were pronounced, though he was unable to do much for them, but his sympathies for small farmers and small-town America were clouded by his admiration for people who knew how to think big and make money on a big scale. The United States was entering into a period not unlike that of the stock market boom of the 1980s or the great "dot.com" boom of the mid-1990s, in which those who were ruthless, clever, and knew how to swim with the tide would make (and sometimes lose) vast fortunes and live on a scale of lavish consumption and display that European royalty could only envy. Like President Clinton in our own times, Grant, having succeeded beyond his dreams, enjoyed the company of the very rich, the "movers and shakers" in the world of big money, and although he was president, he and Mrs. Grant were very conscious of not being among them. Like any president, Grant could do many things to help them, however—in that sense if in no other, the 1870s were no different from our own age. The concept of "conflict of interest" was less highly developed back then—Lincoln, despite his saintliness, was a successful lawyer for the railroads and would have been by no means a poor man, had it not been for Mrs. Lincoln's crazed shopping sprees—and Grant tended to take the view that as a victorious general he was owed a certain style of life.

Then as now victorious American generals expected to be taken care of for life, and Grant was no exception. Nowadays they join the boards of major corporations and head think tanks and foundations; then they accepted outright gifts from grateful citizens and remunerative railway directorships. Having moved virtually straight from the army to the White House, Grant had not had an opportunity to cash in on his victories. Later, when the Grants went on their famous world tour, it did not escape their attention that victorious English generals had been rewarded far more lavishly. John Churchill was created Duke of Marlborough for his victories over Louis XIV and given Blenheim Palace and enough money to support it. Wellington was not only made a duke but given innumerable estates, a great house on Piccadilly at Hyde Park Corner, and a substantial fortune for his victory over Napoleon. By comparison the Grants felt themselves to be very modestly rewarded indeed, particularly since they liked to hobnob with the very richest of the new rich. Galena and (oddly enough) Philadelphia had chipped in with homes for the Grants, but they were far from well off and would be still less so when Grant left the White House.

One reason, therefore, why Grant stayed for two terms as president (and later made an unsuccessful bid for a third) was that the Grants had no

The Grant family in Washington: Julia, Fred, Nellie, Ulysses, Ulysses Jr., Jesse

concrete plans for the future after he left the White House. It was not so much that Grant *enjoyed* being president—he had had none of the fierce presidential ambition that motivates so many who seek the office, and indeed, in a very real sense, the office sought *him*, not the other way round—but he had nothing much else in mind, and once he was settled in, began to think of the White House as his home. It was large, run like a military

MICHAEL KORDA

Grant being sworn in for his second term as president

establishment, furnished richly enough to satisfy Mrs. Grant, and could provide roast turkey at every meal—the only meat Grant ate with anything approaching enthusiasm.

The job of being president he approached with less enthusiasm. It is perhaps one of the real misfortunes of the Grant administration that John A. Rawlins, his aide from Galena and now secretary of war, who had fallen out with Grant during the war, shocked by the growing casualties after the Wilderness, was already a very sick man, suffering from tuberculosis in an age when that was still an incurable disease. Had Grant been surrounded, supported, protected, advised, and "coached," as modern presidents are, by a team of advisers under Rawlins's eagle eye, his presidency might have succeeded better than it did. Just as Rawlins, when he had been well, and close to Grant, had mostly been able to keep him from the bottle (and shield him from the consequences when he managed to avoid Rawlins's vigilance) during the war, so Rawlins in the White House might have been able to protect the president from his natural inability to distinguish cheats, sharpers, thieves, and con artists from honest men. Though in many respects shrewd and thoughtful, Grant was a total innocent when it came to anything involving money, and being almost supernaturally honest himself, he found it difficult to detect dishonesty in others. Besides, he was enormously loyal. He often managed to ignore proof of wrongdoing even when it was brought to him.

These are not the ideal characteristics for a president of the United States, and in the absence of a personality as forceful as Rawlins (who died in 1869, in the first year of Grant's presidency), Grant was left pretty much to his own devices in a White House that was, by modern standards, chaotic and open to an endless crowd of office seekers, admirers, and total strangers. Lincoln had thrived on this kind of thing—he was, after all, a natural politician—but Grant was an army man and needed the kind of staff and efficiency that surrounded his headquarters in the field. It didn't help that he had been nominated for the presidency unanimously, or that he had run for the presidency without making speeches or leaving his new home in Galena. He had never been called upon to define what he wanted to accomplish as president, and his fame and status as a great man and a four-star general were such that practically nobody felt entitled to question him on the matter. His silence made it appear to most people that he was deep in thought or busy formulating plans, but for the most part that was an illusion, although not a deliberate one. Grant certainly desired to produce "peace," "prosperity," "harmony," and the reintegration of the South into the American body politic on terms that protected the former slaves (now called "freedmen") without necessarily making them equal to whites, but he had no idea how to go about achieving these aims.

No less an authority than the historian Allan Nevins summed up Grant's presidency by remarking on "his vast ignorance of civil affairs, economics and his tendency to look upon the presidency as a reward, not a responsibility,"[1] and there is no denying the truth of this, but one must add to it an unfortunate tendency to pursue with the utmost tenacity ideas that had been planted in his head by others and made no sense in the first place. Grant astonished his own cabinet, his own party, and almost everybody who mattered in the U.S. Senate by a politically doomed plan to annex the island of Santo Domingo (later the Dominican Republic) to the United States (he would not be the last American president to get into trouble in the Caribbean). Santo Domingo was weak, split among rival factions, and up for grabs, and once Grant's attention had been directed toward it, he was moved both by a mild sense of imperialism, a late-blooming case, as it were, of Manifest Destiny (although he did not propose to conquer Santo Domingo so much as to buy it), and by the belief that it might absorb perhaps as many as four million American blacks. At one stroke, he imagined, America's position in the Caribbean would be made secure, American investment and ingenuity would turn Santo Domingo into a paying proposition, and the problem of what to do with (and about) the freed slaves in the South would be solved. There was not the slightest enthusiasm for the idea anywhere, as it turned out, except among those Dominican political figures who were eager to sell the country to the highest bidder. Radical Republican senators raised strong objections to the idea of suppressing one of the few existing black republics, American blacks showed no more enthusiasm for the idea of being transplanted to a Caribbean island than they had for being shipped en masse to Liberia—to the extent that they were consulted about it—and hardly anybody wanted to add a black American territory (or, eventually, even less desirable, a state) to the Union. Most vehemently opposed to annexation was the formidable Sen. Charles Sumner of Massachusetts, chairman of the Senate Foreign Relations Committee, whose firm abolitionist beliefs went back long before the Civil War, when he had been savagely beaten with a cane at his seat in the Senate by Preston Brooks, a member of the House from South Carolina, because of his fierce opposition to slavery, and became thereafter both a martyr and a hero to the cause of black rights.

Grant fought this battle to the bitter end, and he lost it. Nor was he a good loser. As Nevins put it, Grant suffered from "his lack of magnanimity, for despite the Appomattox legend, he bore grudges and was a vengeful hater." He became Sumner's sworn enemy, and Sumner—being one of the most respected, even venerated, of Radical Republicans—was a poor choice of enemy. It was not so much that Grant was "a vengeful hater," true though that was, but that he remained thin-skinned, sensitive, and burdened with the inferiority complex of a boy who had been brought up by harsh and distant parents, made fun of at school, been passed over for promotion in the army, failed at every attempt to make money or improve his situation, and eventually settled into life as a clerk in his father's store and the town drunk until the Civil War came along and saved him. He was deeply conscious of the gaps in his education and resentful of any perceived slight. A patrician New Englander, a Harvard man, wealthy, imperious and formidably well read, Sumner was just the man to make Grant conscious of his own shortcomings, and Sumner's opposition to the Santo Domingo scheme was merely the straw that broke the camel's back.[2]

Photographs of Grant in the White House are a painful contrast with those taken of him as a general—he looks puffy, peevish, unfocused; and his civilian suits, obviously meant to be the height of fashion, merely seem pretentious and ill fitting—he doesn't look nearly as comfortable in them as he did in uniform. His hair is slicked back and his shoes look like something a farmer might wear to milk the cows, rather than those of an elegantly dressed politician. There is something about his expression that is at once furtive and depressed, like somebody who is carrying out an imposture or has stumbled into a place where he doesn't belong—say the drawing room of a club of which he is not a member.

The truth is that Grant looks lost, and of course in a certain sense he was. Despite the fact that the citizens of Philadelphia had given the Grants a home, as well as those of Galena, Grant was stuck in the White House, beset with problems he couldn't solve by ordering an attack.

ULYSSES S. GRANT

He had his successes, to give him his due. He resolved the complex set of problems that was endangering relationships with Great Britain, in part due to his own determination to remain calm, in part due to Hamilton Fish's common sense, understanding of diplomacy, and ability to pacify the Senate Committee on Foreign Relations, even the formidable Sumner, who, like many New Englanders, was a confirmed Anglophobe. Appeasing Great Britain was not by any means a popular move in the latter part of the nineteenth century, particularly in New England, where the battles of Lexington, Concord, and Bunker Hill had taken place less than a hundred years before and were still deeply etched in people's memories, as if the Redcoats might reappear at any moment. The feeling was made more acute in the minds of Massachusetts politicians by the increasing presence of large numbers of Irish, whose hatred of the English was bred into their bones, as a voting block.

The issues that had arisen between the United States and the United Kingdom had escalated during the Civil War, exacerbated by the construction in English shipyards of a number of Confederate commerce raiders and blockade runners, which had inflicted major damage on American shipping. Some of these ships were not only built in the United Kingdom but partly manned by British crews. Preposterous sums were being suggested in Congress as "damages" to be paid by the British, Sumner's being an eye-popping two billion five hundred million dollars. In addition to this there were such issues as disputed fishery rights (again significant in Sumner's New England, but not to an Ohio/Illinois man like Grant), Confederate debts, and the growing belief among Radical Republicans that Canada should be annexed, partly to punish the United Kingdom and partly because it seemed obvious to New Englanders, as it had one hundred years earlier, that the Canadians would rather be governed from Washington than from London. However much Grant wanted to annex Santo Domingo, he was not remotely interested in annexing Canada to please Senator Sumner; he doubted that the Canadians wanted to become Americans (they had stoutly—and successfully—resisted an American invasion during the Revolutionary War); and at all costs he didn't want to provoke a war with Britain, then the world's dominant superpower. In the end, by artful diplomacy, by calming down the rhetoric over Canada, and by the then-revolutionary innovation of submitting America's claims to international arbitration in Geneva, Grant managed to achieve a settlement with the United Kingdom that left both countries more or less satisfied and would serve as a model for resolving future international disputes. As a result of this Grant developed a reputation in Europe and the rest of the world rather resembling that of Woodrow Wilson in 1918, as a great statesman who could rise above mere national political concerns—very gratifying, no doubt, but not the best way of winning elections in the United States.

What did in Grant's reputation as a president, however (and continues to do so today whenever journalists and historians are drawing up lists of the best presidents vs. the worst ones), was the depression of 1873, which ushered in a long period of unemployment and distress, made politically more damaging by accusations that the president's wealthy friends were making money out of it (comparisons to the economy in 2003, as this book was being written, will come naturally to mind). Even in his first term there were signs that the American economy was faltering, and it cannot be said that Grant ignored the issue, innocent as he may have been of what is now called "economics." His chief concern was with the question of whether paper dollars (which came to be called "greenbacks" during the Civil War) should be redeemable in specie—that is, gold—partially in specie, or not in specie at all. Since this question was still perplexing Winston Churchill as chancellor of the Exchequer in Great Britain in the 1920s, and Franklin D. Roosevelt in the 1930s, it is hardly surprising that Grant was stumped by it and changed his mind frequently. Since the war

The Green Room in the Grant White House, with portrait of Grant

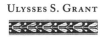

State dining room in the Grant White House

had been fought, as all wars are, by printing large amounts of paper money in the expectation that victory would enable whoever was in charge of things at some later date (hopefully somebody else) to sort matters out, the aftermath, apart from a huge national debt, was an awful lot of doubtful paper money floating about, and not enough gold. Of course things were simpler, as they always are, on the losing side—Confederate paper money became worthless long before Appomattox—but in the United States it was obviously vital to peg the dollar to some acceptable value, gold being the traditional one.

It was Grant's bad luck, given his ignorance of economics, to have to listen to both sides of a monetary discussion that doubtless bored and confused him (Churchill and Roosevelt would be just as bored and confused when their time came), and his tragedy that he was beginning to see himself as one of the "haves" rather than as one of the "have-nots." He had already been bitten by the gold bug before, when, under the false impression that he understood fiscal policy, he fell under the sway of Jay Gould and James Fisk, Jr., two sleazy financial speculators who would have been right at home on Wall Street in the 1990s. Gould and Fisk wanted to "corner" the market in gold and tried over many dinners and in many private dining cars to persuade the president of the importance of the government's buying gold rather than selling it. In the end, however, during the autumn of 1869, Grant changed his mind just when they thought they had him securely on the hook, setting off a gold panic that ruined many people in the financial world and causing what we would now call a "minirecession," in addition to costing him one member of his cabinet and exposing to the world the possibility that Julia Grant herself and some of her relatives may have been involved in, and profited from, the attempts to manipulate the price of gold.

In 1873 the failure of Jay Cooke & Co., a prominent banking firm, precipitated a crash, followed by a protracted, full-blown depression, leaving the country in a mess from which Grant was unable to extricate it and in which his own fortune, such as it was, would soon be consumed. Grant's presidency was to end in a welter of scandals, none of them directly connected to Grant, but most of them the result of his engaging, but mistaken, loyalty to people who had served in the Grand Army of the Republic during the war, or fast-talking, high-living rogues, or friends, or members of his own or his official or Julia's family. The names of the scandals alone give some clue to the kind of thing that darkened his final years in the White House—the Whisky Scandal (having to do with the sale of whiskey on a large and remunerative scale without federal tax stamps), and the Indian Trader's Post Scandal (having to do with the sale and the partitioning of the profits of the lucrative appointments of government trading posts on Indian reservations). A pattern of grift and graft ran through the Grant administration, and though the president was one of the few major figures not to profit from it, he nevertheless seemed unable to do anything to stop it, and he was unwilling to listen to evidence against those he liked or trusted.

It did not help that nobody was happy with the chaos and disarray and sheer brutality of events in the former Confederate states. Under military government blacks began to play a role proportional to their number in state legislatures, but as the states gradually escaped from what they described as "carpetbagger" government, the black freedmen were systematically disenfranchised and prevented from voting by organized campaigns of violence, murder, and lynching, in which the nascent Ku Klux Klan played a large role. In very short order, de facto racial segregation, sharecropping, and political impotence enforced by whites became the substitute for slavery in the South.

Grant was unwilling—again very much like Ike less than a hundred years later—to use federal force to defend the rights of blacks or to challenge the Southern status quo—Grant had won the Civil War but had no interest in refighting it—and at the same time he had no wish to reward former Confederates or unreconstructed racists. He preferred to get the army out of there and leave the Southern states to their own devices, in the hope that time and political realities would produce some form of amelioration of the Southern racial situation without necessarily making blacks the equal of whites. This was, it goes without saying, apostasy to Republicans like Charles Sumner, old abolitionists who could still be stirred by the mention of John Brown, but it seemed like plain common sense to Grant and indeed to much of the country. The destruction of slavery, Grant would later tell that supreme political realist, German chancellor Bismarck, was necessary to end the rebellion and defeat the South, but like most white Americans for the next hundred years, Grant was unwilling to take the next step and accept the former slaves as equals or force the former Confederate states to do so.

(It was typical of the era that the few blacks to enter West Point as cadets, having surmounted almost impossible difficulties intended to keep them out, were persecuted and treated with contempt by the student body and the officer instructors alike. Here was an area in which even a word from Grant might have ended the campaign of discrimination, but it was not forthcoming, and it would not be until the mid–twentieth century that the experiment was tried again.)

Perhaps the brightest spot in Grant's eight years as president was the marriage of his beloved daughter, Nellie, in the White House. Nellie, to judge from photographs, was pretty, intelligent, and good-humored—she was lucky to have inherited her looks more from her father than her mother—and the Grants were especially gratified when she fell in love with a handsome, elegant young Englishman with the almost too perfect name of Algernon Sartoris, whom she met on a transatlantic steamer. Sartoris was a nephew of the great actress Fanny Kemble,

Nellie Grant

and his family was prosperous, with just enough connections to the aristocracy to thrill the Grants, or at any rate to thrill Julia and Nellie. One might have thought that Sartoris would have been pleased to have wooed and won the daughter of the president of the United States, but the Grants appear to have been more dazzled by him than he was by them. In any event, despite a glamorous wedding in the White House, the marriage, except for the fact that it produced four children, was a flop. Sartoris seems to have been a philanderer, a cheat, and a drunk, and reading between the lines may have been under the impression that Grant was wealthy, as well as a famous general and president—the discovery by Sartoris, when it was too late, that he had not married into money may have been partly responsible for the marital problems, but in any case Nellie would eventually return to the United States with her children, though many years were to pass before she could get a divorce.

Whatever else can be said of Grant, he was the most indulgent of parents—clearly his own harsh childhood had taught him something, and he seems to have found in his family life a happiness that eluded him in his public life.

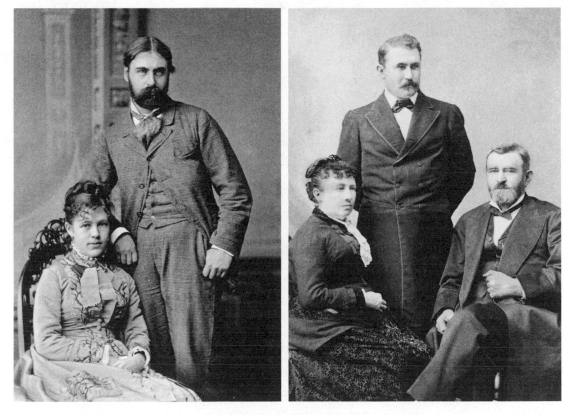

Left: *Nellie Grant and Algernon Sartoris*. Right: *Julia and Ulysses with son Frederick (standing)*

The Grant family

Still, taking it all in all, his presidency was not the failure that historians have portrayed it. He kept America out of two wars; if his attempt to annex Santo Domingo was foolish, his refusal to try to annex Canada was courageous and smart, and the failure of the economy was perhaps beyond his control or anybody else's. The corruption that marked the Grant administration was brought about by his innocence and his trust in other people, not by any desire for personal gain, and was, in any case, endemic to what came to be called the "Gilded Age." The United States was growing too fast, in too many different directions at once, and the inevitable consequence was corruption and an unstable economy, and it would have taken a more astute man than Grant to slow things down or clean them up.

All the same the middle period of Grant's life is disappointing. Appomattox was his greatest moment—the years afterward, despite two terms as president, show him as a man drifting into late middle age without a sense of direction, eager to become a wealthy and respected bourgeois but congenitally ill equipped to do so. Failure as a young man had honed and hardened him for war, and war, when it came, made him a hero; now another long and difficult period of failure would offer him another opportunity for heroism. Not too many people are given two chances to be a hero in a lifetime. Although Grant could not have guessed it, as he prepared to leave the White House, he was to be one of them.

ULYSSES S. GRANT

CHAPTER

9

In 1877 retiring presidents did not have the benefits that they do today—no "presidential library" to build and administer, no office and staff at government expense, no Secret Service protection, no generous pension. The Founding Fathers had intended that presidents should return to everyday life, hopefully to their farms or plantations, as ordinary citizens, and certainly the first presidents did so, following the example set by Washington. Grant, however, was still a comparatively young man and had no equivalent of Mount Vernon or Monticello to hold him. He had invested a good deal of money in a horse farm built on Dent land near St. Louis, but as usual, that had turned out to be a bad investment, and in any case he was hardly likely to spend the rest of his life raising trotters. Galena held no attractions for him, and he and Mrs. Grant knew hardly anyone in Philadelphia, in both of which places they had been given houses by a grateful public.

Grant solved the problem, initially, by the traditional American solution to retirement: taking a world tour.

How curious Grant was about the rest of the world is hard to say, but the rest of the world was intensely curious about *him*, so that it became like a royal tour, in which the Grants were the sightseeing attraction, rather than the scenery or famous monuments. In the United States, though his popularity was still immense, he was nevertheless, for many people, a

Republican former president, which is to say that there *were* those who disagreed with his actions as a political figure though not as a general. Abroad he was simply a celebrity, the first American president to travel around the world offering himself up to the millions who saw him and Mrs. Grant as if they were part of P. T. Barnum's circus and freak show.

Their tour around the world was of unprecedented length—nearly two years—partly because travel in those days was slow, and partly because Grant had shrewdly calculated that the longer they stayed away from the United States, the more curiosity there would be to greet them when they got home. Two years is a long time in politics—long enough for people to become fed up with President Rutherford B. Hayes and look back on Grant's presidency as a golden age. Or so, no doubt, Grant hoped.

In England the Grants were treated like royalty, even *by* royalty, and given the unusual honor of a private dinner with Queen Victoria at Windsor, marred only by the embarrassing insistence of their bumptious son Jesse that he sit at the queen's table, to which her majesty finally consented though she found the young man ill-mannered and pushy. The Grants were given dinners by the Prince of Wales (the future Edward VII), the Duke of Devonshire, and the second Duke of Wellington, as well as fulsome public banquets, including one at the Guildhall in which the Lord Mayor of London presented him with the freedom of the City of London, and in general feted him from one end of the realm to the other. Perhaps most extraordinary were the enormous number of English workingmen who turned out to greet Grant, seeing in him not only the man who had destroyed slavery but who represented something that was still unthinkable in Great Britain—the rise of a former leather tanner and shop clerk to four-star general and president. Grant seems to have been overwhelmed and bewildered by his popularity among "the working classes," but it was a fact, and he came to accept it. His inarticulateness helped too—the fact that he did not make long, windy speeches appealed to them; he was "a man of few words," and many people who got close enough to him remarked on his robust physique, his apparent physical strength, and his big, blunt-fingered workingman's hands—hands that had at one time plowed fields, felled trees, cut hay, harnessed horses, and raised pigs, however unsuccessfully.

His reception in France and in Italy was hardly less extraordinary. The Grants saw all the sights—including Pompei—then went on to Egypt, and from there to the Holy Land (at the time still a Turkish province), to Constantinople, back to Italy, and on to Holland, Denmark, Norway, Russia, Germany, and Spain. Grant met Czar Alexander II, Bismarck, Pope Leo XIII, and French premier Georges Clemenceau—everybody who mattered

President and Mrs. Grant in Memphis, Egypt

The Grants (center) *in Egypt*

in Europe. Then, after a trip back to England, the Grants set out for India, China, and Japan via the Suez Canal: two well-fed, solidly built Americans with an apparently inextinguishable appetite for food and travel—the prototypes for generations to come of American world travelers. The farther Grant journeyed from his native land, the more he was treated as a distinguished world figure, the peak being reached when he was presented to the emperor Meiji of Japan, who actually shook hands with Grant, something no Japanese emperor had ever done before with anyone, native or foreign.

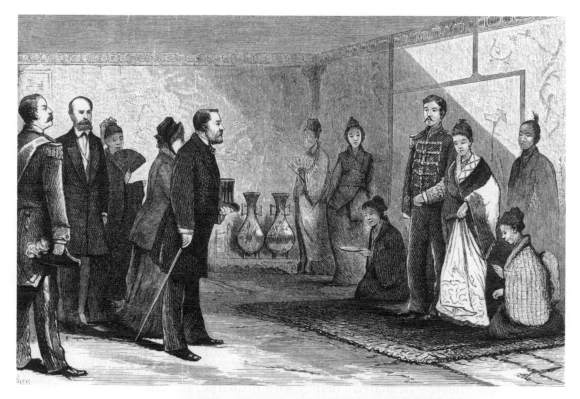

Grant becomes the first man ever to shake the hand of the Japanese emperor

Through it all Grant ate, read, and gazed at the sights placidly, apparently beyond boredom. There were rumors that from time to time he got drunk—who could blame him?—and in India the viceroy, Lord Lytton, whose account of an evening with the Grants is quoted in McFeely's biography of Grant, claimed that it took six British sailors to haul a drunken Grant away from a shipboard reception at which he had pinched young ladies' bottoms and indecently ogled their *decolletés*, and place him in another room where he satiated his lust on Mrs. Grant, then threw up on her. Lytton was a man who enjoyed telling tall tales and, no shrinking violet himself when it came to the ladies, he was probably exaggerating. Photographs of Mrs. Grant at the time make the incident as he describes it seem unlikely—given her bulk and obvious strength, she could surely have resisted the general, and from what we know of her the suggestion that she would have had sexual intercourse with him in any kind of public view seems very improbable. That Grant was drinking again, however, is undeniable—he shared a brandy with Bismarck, and champagne with the Prince of Wales, and endless wines were served at the innumerable banquets that were held in the Grants' honor. It would have been very difficult for him to refuse a drink or a toast without being rude, and with Grant one drink led to another. By the time Grant reached India he had been traveling for almost a year and a half, and like many another tourist, the charm of seeing yet another famous monument in the company of his wife may have worn thin by then.

Since Lord Lytton's is, so far as I know, the only allegation of sexual impropriety against Grant, I am prepared to dismiss it or at least overlook it, but the drinking is more of a problem. For Grant sobriety was all important—the lack of it was a sign that he was getting restless, as indeed he must have been.[1]

No sooner were the Grants back in the United States than he began to explore the possibility of being nominated by the Republicans for a third term. Whether or not Grant was conscious of it himself, he needed to perform a difficult balancing act—he had to appear everywhere, making himself look electable, but he must never be seen to be seeking the nomination. Whether it had been a good idea for him to spend two years traveling abroad is a difficult question. On the one hand it kept him out of the country, while the press sent back flattering reports of his tour, but on the other he was out of the loop of Republican politics and obliged to travel around the United States accepting applause at public functions without actually saying anything or explaining what he would do in the White House if the party and the public persuaded him to run.

Grant in Key West, Florida, 1880

Besides, 1880 was not 1869. The Republican Party had as good as conceded the South to the Democrats by failing to stand up for black voters, and while respect for Grant still ran high among Republicans of every stripe and the mass of voters, there were new issues confronting the nation, and Grant's victories, while still admired, were not sufficient to compensate for the absence on his part of any concrete program. A new generation of voters was coming of age, in any case, for whom Grant's victories were their fathers' battles.

Even so, Grant managed to get a respectable number of votes—he was in the lead on the first ballot at Chicago—and he might very well have swept to the nomination on the enthusiasm of the delegates had he condescended to visit the convention hall, as Julia urged him to do. But he could not or would not play that kind of role; it was simply not in his nature, and as a result he lost the nomination to James A. Garfield, who handily defeated the Democratic candidate, Gen. Winfield Scott Hancock—the man who broke Pickett's charge on the third day of Gettysburg, and against whom Grant nursed a burning resentment.

Grant made his peace with Garfield, and most (but not all) of those Republicans who had failed to support him, but he did not get a seat in Garfield's cabinet or even an ambassadorship. He was left with nothing much to do and not much money to do it with. A visit to Mexico, a country he had been fond of even when fighting there, offered the possibility of playing a major role in an American plan to build railways there, but although Grant had set himself up with a handsome residence on East Sixty-sixth Street in New York City and an office on Wall Street in expectation of success, his hopes as a railway entrepreneur eventually came to nothing, leaving him once again with the difficult problem of what to do, and the even more difficult one of how to make money. The Grants liked to live in style, and in a manner fitting for a former president who moved in wealthy financial circles, with hardly any income to support it. If a cabinet post, an ambassadorship, or the Mexican railways would not do the trick, Grant would have to find something else.

Opportunity appeared from, of all people, one of his sons, Ulysses Grant, Jr. Buck Grant had made an advantageous marriage and gone into business on Wall Street with capital provided by his father-in-law. His partner was Ferdinand Ward, a plausible and attractive young man with a certain business flair. Buck Grant, like his father, was a true believer in other people's business schemes, and it seemed to him logical for his father to sink his remaining capital into the firm of Grant & Ward and make a fortune. It is a measure of Grant's enduring—and endearing—naïveté that he was persuaded to attempt to become a Wall Street tycoon—few things were as clear as Grant's poor judgment about money and schemes to make money—yet that is precisely what he decided to do.

Buck was an innocent dupe, Ward a clever con man. And the outcome was predictable. Ward's idea was to use Grant as a front to attract investments from Civil War veterans. With Grant's name on the letterhead the money flowed in, and Ward used each new investment to show a profit to the previous investors—what would come to be known as a Ponzi scheme. In the meantime Ward was stealing the partnership blind, which became only too shockingly apparent when Ward had to admit, in May 1884, that the firm was technically bankrupt. In one last burst of confidence trickery, Ward persuaded Grant to borrow $150,000 from the formidable William Vanderbilt, which Vanderbilt agreed to on Grant's personal word. Then Ward vanished into protracted litigation and prison along with Vanderbilt's $150,000, and Grant was left holding the bag, bankrupt, an object of scorn or pity (depending on which party you belonged to), by any standards ruined. No American ex-president had ever fallen so low, and except for Harding and Nixon, none ever would again.

CHAPTER

10

R uined and saddled with debt, Grant was, in some respects, back where he had started when he was working at the leather shop in Galena. As always in his extraordinary life, however, a chance to rise was once again about to present itself. Once again he would need to go through pain and suffering; once again he would overcome them to win glory. This time the weapon would be the pen, not the sword.

In the aftermath of the failure of Grant & Ward, Grant had rather reluctantly agreed to write an account of Shiloh for *Century Magazine*, for a fee of five hundred dollars; more articles were called for, and it gradually dawned on the editor of the *Century* that a book might eventually come of all this. It also dawned on a former Confederate soldier, Samuel Clemens (more famous under his writing name of Mark Twain), that such a book would sell. Clemens was a publisher as well as a humorist and writer, and owned his own publishing house, Charles L. Webster & Co., having discovered that he could make more money by selling his books door-to-door than through conventional publishers and booksellers, who even then were thought to be behind the times when it came to marketing their product. Clemens knew the general slightly and dropped in to see him at East Sixty-sixth Street—Clemens was a celebrity, the late-nineteenth-century equivalent of a major talk-show host, as well as a famous writer, and he had the rare gift of being able to make Grant smile, so no doubt he was welcome. He was also a man with a vision, and proposed to secure for Grant at least $25,000 for his war memoirs, against very favorable royalty terms that would make him, once again, a rich man. Grant typically countered with the loyalty that he owed to the *Century* people, but Clemens promised him they would never match his offer or come up with anything like it, and he was proved right. The head of the *Century*—typically of a publisher—declared rather stuffily that he would never guarantee the sale of 25,000 copies of any book ever written, and Clemens, therefore, got Grant's memoirs, thus making Grant the first in a long line of presidents who would secure their financial future with a book deal, including Truman, Eisenhower, Nixon, and Bill Clinton.

Unlike most of them, however, Grant aimed to write his book himself, without the help of a "ghostwriter." Every word would be his. Clemens was shrewd enough to know that Grant's prose was one of his greatest strengths. His letters and dispatches, however hastily written, were always models of brevity, clarity, and simplicity—he had only to keep at it steadily to produce a major bestseller.[1]

But there was one problem. Grant had been suffering for some time from a pain in the throat, accompanied by difficulty in swallowing. He had experienced it shortly after the collapse of Grant & Ward, when his mind had been on other things—disgrace and ruin—and had paid, at first, little attention to it. It was diagnosed as a cold, but the pain persisted long after the cold should have gone away, and as throat specialists were called in, the diagnosis became clearer and more dire—Grant was suffering from cancer of the throat, an incurable disease in the age before radiation and chemotherapy, in effect a death sentence, and a slow and painful death at that.

Grant took the news stoically, but he was determined to finish his book before he died. The writing was laborious, slow work, and became daily more difficult as Grant's cancer spread, rendering it impossible for him to swallow and eventually depriving him of his voice. Still he labored on, day after day, convinced by now that it was the only way in which his debts could be settled and Julia and his family provided for.

What fate had in store for Grant was a race against time—a race against death, really—and the struggle wiped away every trace of the man who had twice been president and tried so hard to get a third term without actually asking for it. That Grant, overweight, puffy-faced, overdressed in clothes that didn't suit him, the Grant who had yearned to be a Wall Street tycoon or a Mexican railways baron, and who had traveled around the world accepting as his due the homage of huge crowds of ordinary people and the company of crowned heads, was now burned away day by day, bit by bit, by pain, suffering, and remorselessly hard work under overwhelming pressure. Photographs taken of Grant in his illness show the flesh pared away, the strong bones reappearing in his face, the eyes once again melancholy but focused with disconcerting concentration on the object of his attention, as they had once been in battle. In these photographs Grant, the heroic young officer of the Mexican War; Grant, the fledgling colonel of the Illinois Volunteers who surrounded Buckner at Fort Donelson; Grant, the victor of Shiloh, Vicksburg, and the long, bloody struggle against Lee in 1864 and 1865, reappears as if the other Grant had never existed. He was, in fact, at war again, not only in his head, as day by day he reconstructed with phenomenal exactitude and in succinct lapidary prose the history of his wars and his battles, but also in his heart, as he took the measure of the cancer that was killing him; figured out how much pain he could bear and how much morphine he could afford to take before it clouded his mind and stopped his writing; drew on his own strength, courage, and stubborn determination to fight his last battle, in which the only victory would be to complete his book before death took him.

Grant began his task late in 1884 and finished it in July 1885—an amazing and Herculean labor. At first he dictated, but then, as his ability to speak deteriorated, he took to writing on lined yellow legal pads with a pencil, in his clear, firm script. He did not have an army of researchers and draft writers, like Winston Churchill for instance. He sat on his porch, if the weather allowed it, and wrote away industriously, often watched by sightseers who had come to see the great man die. The Grants had been obliged to sell their seaside cottage in New Jersey, and took a small house at Mount McGregor, near Saratoga Springs, New York. There Grant can be seen, in numerous photographs, dressed in a dark, frock-coated suit with silk lapels, a black silk top hat on his head and a white napkin or towel wrapped around his throat, resolutely writing.

He knew he was dying, and very shortly the country knew it, too. Visitors came to pay their last respects, crowds of tourists came up from Saratoga Springs to stand and gawk at Grant; he was, as was so often the case in his life, on public display. In an age when deathbed scenes were popular and apt to be protracted, and when people died at home rather than in a hospital, Grant's was perhaps the biggest and longest deathbed

Grant at Mount McGregor, June 1885

Grant surrounded by his family

scene of all, and through it he kept working, surrounded by his family, and receiving occasional visitors.

It was a national drama of unprecedented proportions, and as his health declined and pain began to overwhelm his defenses, his enemies and his detractors fell away, one by one. Those who had thought he was wasteful of his men's lives in the war, those who had opposed his presidency, those who had lost their life's savings in the crash and depression that darkened his second term in office, or had unwisely invested their money in Grant & Ward because of his name, came to forgive him—dying made him again what he had once been, a national hero.

He finished the last chapter only a week or so before his death and was still struggling with questions about the maps and the proofs when death was almost ready to take him. On his own terms, and in his own way, he had fought death and won.

*Grant working on
his book toward
the end of his life*

Now that it was too late, final honors poured in—Congress passed a bill restoring him to his rank in the army (he had had to resign in order to run for president); encomiums filled the newspapers; people of every rank, from all over the world, sent letters and cards; but Grant was past all that. He had finished his book, and now he was ready, perhaps even impatient, to die.

He would never know it, of course, but the book would indeed save the Grants—it would earn more than $450,000 in royalties, an immense sum for the day, but one that would have to be multiplied by twenty or more to give an idea of it in comparable modern terms. Sold door to door in several different editions, it became the biggest bestseller in American history, excluding the Bible.

All over the United States in the late nineteenth century, in the simplest of homes and farmhouses, one could always count on finding two books, the Bible and Grant's *Memoirs*, side by side, on a shelf or on the mantelpiece, its penultimate words, "Let us have peace," representing, so very clearly, the deepest feelings of America's most successful general.

Grant's deathbed

The funeral cortege

*Grant's burial in the Grant National Memorial,
Morningside Heights, New York City*

Epilogue

WHY GRANT?

There are many biographies of Grant, so many that it seems to be something of a minor industry; some of them, like William S. McFeely's *Grant*, are works of literature, many others more humdrum or narrowly military in interest. But from time to time it is necessary to remind Americans about Grant, first of all because his is a kind of real-life Horatio Alger story, exactly the one that foreigners have always wanted to believe about American life (hence the immense crowds that greeted Grant on his world tour) and that Americans want to believe about themselves. He came from a humble background; he had a harsh childhood; success eluded him at every turn no matter how hard he worked; then, all of a sudden, he rose to fame, to command, to power, to victory; then managed as few other people could have done (perhaps only Lincoln) to end the Civil War on a note of grace; served two terms as president; and ended his life by writing the most successful book in American literature. He was, in his lifetime, living proof of a substantial element of the American dream, and continued to be for many years after his death.

His presidency was clearly flawed, but what he sought as president—peace, prosperity, the binding together of North and South despite the wounds of four years of civil war, and good relations with foreign powers—

was sought after by most Americans then and continues to be today. In domestic politics Grant sought to achieve fairness and failed, certainly in the case of black Americans; in foreign policy he avoided a bullying or a moralistic tone and refrained from the use of military force. Like Winston Churchill he believed that "It is better to jaw, jaw, jaw than to war, war, war," and his decision to submit American claims against the United Kingdom to international arbitration and not to encourage the annexation of Canada shows a degree of common sense that we might well wish to see repeated in our own day.

As a general Grant defined for all time the American way of winning a war, from which, nearly 150 years later, we deviate at our own risk. Grant understood better than anyone that, first of all, any American war must be firmly based on the support of the American people and have an essentially moral base, and that the best way for the United States to win a war was to use to the full its great industrial strength and its reserves of manpower—and to apply them both unhesitatingly on the battlefield.

Grant was not a showy general. No admirer of Napoleon, he nevertheless had to some degree what Napoleon called *"le coup d'oeil de génie,"* the quick glance of genius, by which Napoleon meant the ability to see at once on the battlefield where the enemy's weakness lay and how to exploit it with one unexpected blow. Grant, like Napoleon himself, didn't rise to that level every time—at Shiloh he was caught off guard and fumbled his way through the first day of the battle, to be saved by Johnston's death on the battlefield and Buell's arrival at the last minute with fresh troops—but usually his keen grasp of the enemy's position and its potential weaknesses was remarkable.

Lee had that quality, too, of course, though it failed him at Gettysburg, where he allowed the battle to become a "pounding match," in Wellington's phrase, which, given the enemy's position on high ground with interior lines and Lee's own inferiority in numbers, he could only lose, even though Lee was a better general than Meade. Both Grant and Lee were masters of the quick, surprising movement, the sudden change of plans that, for example, brought Grant's army from north of Richmond to southeast of it, and led to the siege of Petersburg and, eventually, the end of the war.

The war they fought is studied all over the world in staff colleges, still today—indeed German tank commanders like Rommel, Guderian, Manteuffel, and Manstein (and their Soviet equivalents) learned Stonewall Jackson's Shenandoah campaign by heart, so that for them Winchester, Harrisonburg, New Market, Harpers Ferry, Port Republic, and Cross Keys were as familiar as German place names, and the landscape of the Shenandoah Valley was as firmly planted in their minds as that of the Rhine or the Elbe or eastern France. Similarly, in every imaginable language, in military academies all over the world, Grant's capture of Vicksburg, his pursuit of Lee from the Wilderness to Appomattox, and his swift, implacable movements to the left to isolate the Army of Northern Virginia and force Lee's surrender are taught and studied down to the last detail. The machine gun, the tank, the aircraft, the computer and "smart" weaponry have changed the way wars are fought, but not the way they are won. Grant understood topography, the importance of supply lines, the instant judgment of the balance between his own strengths and the enemy's weaknesses, and above all the need to keep his armies moving forward, despite casualties, even when things have gone wrong—that and the simple importance of inflicting greater losses on the enemy than he can sustain, day after day, until he breaks. Grant the boy never retraced his steps. Grant the man did not retreat—he advanced. Generals who do that win wars.

When the United States has succeeded in war, it has been by following Grant's example.

When asked who France's greatest poet was, the nineteenth-century

French literary critic Charles-Augustin Saint-Beuve replied, *"Victor Hugo, hélas."* If I were asked who America's greatest general was, I should have to echo Saint-Beuve: Ulysses S. Grant, alas.

MICHAEL KORDA

Perhaps fortunately for the United States, the nation has never produced an Alexander, a Caesar, or a Napoleon. Washington was a commander of great dignity and fortitude, but retreated his way to victory, abandoning, at one point or another, almost all of America's major cities. Lee was as fierce as Grant, when his blood was up, and one of those rare generals who was as good at defense as attack, and his formidable dignity still impresses Americans 150 years after his surrender at Appomattox. Still we should remember that it was Grant who finally beat him. Of Lee's commanders Longstreet was a kind of Southern Omar Bradley, competent, reliable, a bit cautious, while Jackson was more like a Patton, a master of swift-moving war.

On the Union side Meade was a solid and reliable general, rather like Field Marshal Harold Alexander on the British side in World War II, but hampered by his irascible temper and poor sense of public relations. Both he and Hancock deserved more than they got, from the country and from Grant. In World War II, MacArthur can be thought of as a latter-day McClellan, vain, arrogant, good at public relations, contemptuous of the president, and with one eye fixed on the White House, but Grant is the best of them—Grant and Ike.

Ike was, like Grant, a slow starter whose military career limped along in low gear for years. He missed the fighting in World War I, to his great disappointment, and only got to Europe after it was over as part of the war graves commission. He chafed miserably as General MacArthur's aide in the Philippines, and in the end was promoted to lieutenant colonel only because Gen. George C. Marshall remembered him, from years of inspecting dreary peacetime army bases, as the best bridge player in the

U.S. Army. Like Grant, Ike was no keen student of strategy, and he fumbled the ball badly in North Africa, but he had the rare ability to keep a coalition together, he was a good listener, he understood that the president was more important than any general (a lesson never learned by MacArthur), and above all he knew the importance of bringing overwhelming force against the enemy at his weakest point. Like Grant, too, Ike may not have read Napoleon at West Point—but he had certainly read Grant's memoirs.

Once Ike landed in France, he had to contend with two showier and more flamboyant generals, both prima donnas who believed that the war could be won with one brilliant strategic stroke. George S. Patton wanted to strike southeast deep into Germany, then turn north to cut off Berlin, while Bernard Montgomery was determined to advance to the northeast across Holland, cross the Rhine and occupy the Ruhr, cutting the German army off from its industrial base. Ike, like Grant, was always suspicious of panaceas. In the end he reluctantly turned Patton loose, but kept a tight rein on him (which Patton never forgave), and gave Montgomery a chance to prove his point with the airborne assault on the bridges at Nijmegen and Arnhem (Operation Market-Garden), followed by an armored attack that was supposed to roll over the bridges captured by the airborne troops until Montgomery's army was across the Rhine. Market-Garden failed, and Patton's deep slice into Germany was thwarted by the Battle of the Bulge, the last major German attack in the west. In the end Ike did what he had always planned to do, and just what Grant would have done—he used his superiority in numbers to advance on a broad front, from the Swiss border to Holland, day by day, with no showy tactics or sideshows, inexorably pressing the Germans back and inflicting on them losses they could not afford. It was the Wilderness and the advance on Richmond on a larger scale, and it worked, just as it had for Grant. The German army was better trained, better led, vastly more experienced, and equipped with better weapons, particularly in tanks, but none of it mattered; Ike had the men, and he could replace his weapons thanks to America's industrial might—all he had to do to win the war was to keep moving forward, never retreat, and kill Germans in numbers they could not replace, and eventually they would collapse. And so they did.

Grant would have approved. He would have approved of the fact too that as president Ike was notably unwilling to fight another war. He had seen one, and that was enough for him.

Grant had seen two, and had no nostalgia for the experience. His memoirs are factual, precise, and about as objective as it is possible to be, but there is in them no attempt to portray war as glamorous, or glorious. Glory did not interest Grant. He would have hated Douglas MacArthur's memoirs, and admired Ike's for their modesty and calm tone. Grant would not have loved, like the Air Cav colonel played by Robert Duvall in *Apocalypse Now*, the smell of napalm in the morning (or at any other time). He hated war; the sight of a battlefield gave him no pleasure, and if he fought hard it was to bring the war to an end as quickly as possible. "Next to a battle lost, there is no spectacle more melancholy than a battle won," Wellington said, and Grant would have been the first to agree with him.

I imagine that Grant would have agreed with the "Powell Doctrine" too, which is (or was) that the American armed forces ought to be used only when there is strong civilian support in favor of their use, and then used in overwhelming numbers, bringing America's vast industrial resources and strength to bear on the enemy for a quick, crushing, and complete victory, and then bringing the troops home again as soon as possible. The difficulties of Reconstruction in the South taught Grant—not that he needed teaching—that armies of occupation are no substitute for political thought, and that generals are not necessarily the right people to institute basic political reforms or to reconstruct societies.

Whenever we think about the uses of American power, we would do well to remember Ulysses S. Grant—and to reread his memoirs, which, along with the victory that he won, are his greatest and most lasting legacy to us.

Above all, any politician contemplating the use of force should read Grant before doing so.

RESIDENCE OF GEN. GRANT

ACKNOWLEDGMENTS

I would like to thank particularly James Atlas, for giving me the opportunity to write about Grant, Larry McMurtry and David McCullough for their example and sound advice, and Kevin Kwan for his masterful help in choosing the illustrations. As always, I thank Margaret for her love and patience.

NOTES

A Note on Sources

The list is too long to include in full, but two books I have relied upon, though they are very different in their point of view, have been *Grant* by William S. McFeely (Newtown, Conn.: American Political Biography Press, 1997), and *Meet General Grant* by W. E. Woodward (1928; reprint, New York: Norton, 1965). Indispensable are *The West Point Atlas of American Wars: Volume I, 1689–1900*, edited by Brig. Gen. Vincent J. Esposito (West Point, N.Y., 1995) and *The Papers of Ulysses S. Grant*, edited by John Y. Simon (Carbondale, IL: Southern Illinois University Press, 1967–). Reference must also be made to *The Civil War Battlefield Guide*, 2nd ed., edited by Frances H. Kennedy (Boston: Houghton Mifflin, 1990), *Grant: A Military Commander*, by Sir James Marshall-Cornwall (New York: Barnes & Noble, 1996), and, of course, *Grant's Memoirs and Selected Letters* in the Library of America edition (New York, 1990).

Chapter 1

1. *New York Daily News*, July 9, 2003; Associated Press, July 12, 2003.
2. Information on Grant's tomb is taken mostly from "Grant's Tomb: An Overview" (available at http://www.grantstomb.org/oview1.html), "The Grant Monument Association Update on Grant's Tomb," March 19, 2003 (http://www.morningside-heights.net); and CNN Interactive *U.S. News*, April 27, 1997.
3. "Men Grant Disliked," Ulysses S. Grant home page, http://www.mscomm.com/~ulysses/page140.html.

CHAPTER 2

1. William S. McFeely, *Grant*.
2. W. E. Woodward, *Meet General Grant*. I am indebted to Woodward for much of the information about Grant's childhood. Writing in 1928, Woodward was closer to Grant's time and had an affinity for his subject's early years, and also for those of his future wife.

CHAPTER 3

1. For much of this I have relied on McFeely, who is excellent on the subject of the Dent family.
2. Again, McFeely's is the best account of Grant's military career in the Mexican War.

CHAPTER 4

1. Woodward is an excellent source for Grant's failure as a farmer.

CHAPTER 5

1. McFeely is a superb guide to this complex period of Grant's life.
2. In general, in describing Grant's battles, I have relied on *The West Point Atlas of the American Wars*.
3. As quoted in Woodward.

CHAPTER 6

1. I have used several sources for Vicksburg, in order to try to condense the long and complicated struggle into a short and comprehensible form.

CHAPTER 7

1. There are several differing accounts of Grant's arrival in Washington, and I have combined what seemed to me the most plausible ones (McFeely and Woodward) into a simple narrative.
2. Again, *The West Point Atlas of the American Wars* is the basis for this, and for the rest of the chapter up to Appomattox.

CHAPTER 8

1. Ulysses S. Grant home page.
2. McFeely's is the best account of the Santo Domingo fiasco.

CHAPTER 9

1. McFeely takes a slightly more serious view of Lord Lytton's description of Grant's escapade than I do, but is otherwise excellent on the Grants' world tour.

CHAPTER 10

1. Perhaps the best source for the writing of Grant's memoirs is *General Grant by Matthew Arnold, with a Rejoinder by Mark Twain,* edited by John Y. Simon (Kent, Ohio: Kent State University Press, 1995), who is also responsible for the monumental collection of *The Papers of Ulysses S. Grant* and is surely the dean of Grant scholars.

ILLUSTRATION CREDITS

Grateful acknowledgment for permission to reproduce illustrations is made to the following:

INTERIOR TEXT

American Antiquarian Society, Worcester, Massachusetts, USA/The Bridgeman Art Library: page 123, 124 (bottom), 128, 129, 130, 171 (right)

The Art Archive at Art Resource: page 136

Bultema-Williams Collection at the Ulysses S. Grant Presidential Library: page 12, 15, 19, 120, 157, 195 (top)

CCI/The Art Archive at Art Resource: page 146

Culver Pictures/The Art Archive at Art Resource, New York: page iv, 121, 124 (top), 125, 126, 127, 131, 132, 133, 135, 137, 139, 148–49, 150, 153, 159, 170, 172, 175, 179, 183, 192

Erin Pauwels Collection/The Art Archive at Art Resource: page 134

F&A Archive/The Art Archive at Art Resource: page 163 (left and right)

Gianni Dagli Orti/The Art Archive at Art Resource, New York: page 31

Library of Congress, Prints and Photographs Division: page 24, 49, 56, 113, 117, 166, 171 (left), 180, 194, 195 (bottom)

© Museum of the City of New York, USA/The Bridgeman Art Library: page 1, 196–97

National Archives: page 167

National Portrait Gallery, Smithsonian Institution/Art Resource: page 35, 85, 97, 193

The New York Public Library/Art Resource, New York: page 63, 74–75, 96, 101, 104, 158, 181 (top and bottom), 187, 205

Peter Newark Military Pictures/The Bridgeman Art Library: page 112

© 2013 Stock Sales WGBH/Scala/Art Resource, New York: page 147

Color Insert

Childhood home of Ulysses S. Grant: Library of Congress, Prints and Photographs Division.

Grant home in Galena, Illinois: Library of Congress, Prints and Photographs Division

General Winfield Scott enters Mexico City: National History Museum Mexico City/Gianni Dagli Orti/The Art Archive at Art Resource, New York

Bombardment of Fort Henry, Tennessee: Library of Congress, Prints and Photographs Division

Storming of Fort Donelson by Currier & Ives: Gilder Lehrman Collection, New York, USA/The Bridgeman Art Library

Grant looking over the Battlefield at Fort Donelson by Paul Phillipoteaux: © Chicago History Museum, USA/The Bridgeman Art Library

Storming of Vicksburg: © 2013 Stock Sales WGBH/Scala/Art Resource, New York

Siege of Vicksburg by Angus McBride: Private Collection/© Look and Learn/ The Bridgeman Art Library

Siege of Vicksburg (underlay): Library of Congress, Prints and Photographs Division

Map of Vicksburg and defenses: Culver Pictures/The Art Archive at Art Resource, New York

Battle of Chattanooga: Universal History Archive/UIG/The Bridgeman Art Library

Battle of Lookout Mountain by Kurz and Allison: Culver Pictures/The Art Archive at Art Resource

Battle of Shiloh by Kurz and Allison: © Collection of the New-York Historical Society, USA/The Bridgeman Art Library

Battle of Cold Harbor: Library of Congress, Prints and Photographs Division

Ulysses S. Grant by George P.A. Healy: © Chicago History Museum, USA/The Bridgeman Art Library

Ulysses S. Grant by George P. A. Healy: Newberry Library, Chicago, Illinois, USA/The Bridgeman Art Library

The Peacemakers by George P. A. Healy: Culver Pictures/The Art Archive at Art Resource, New York

General Lee and His Horse "Traveller" Surrenders to General Grant by James Edwin McConnell: Private Collection/© Look and Learn/The Bridgeman Art Library

Lee's Surrender at Appomattox Court House by Tom Lovell: National Geographic Creative/The Bridgeman Art Library

Grant and His Generals on Horseback by E. Boell: Library of Congress, Prints and Photographs Division

Nellie Grant's Wedding in the White House: White House Historical Association

Looking at Wedding Gifts: Library of Congress Prints and Photographs Division

Cartoon of Grant by James A. Wales: The Art Archive at Art Resource, New York

Grant's Tomb: The Museum of the City of New York/Art Resource.

INDEX

Note: An italic *f* indicates the presence of an illustration.

ABOUT THE AUTHOR

Michael Korda is the editor in chief emeritus of Simon & Schuster and is the author, among many other books, of *Ike* and *Charmed Lives*. He lives in Pleasant Valley, New York.